The
Montessori
Homeschooler

Praise for Lynda Apostol and *The Montessori Homeschooler*

"As the founder of a Montessori parenting platform and the Childhood Potential conferences, I've seen thousands of families searching for authentic guidance. In a space filled with surface-level advice, *The Montessori Homeschooler* stands out—it's clear, practical, and deeply respectful of both the child and the parent. Lynda Apostol brings a rare combination of professional expertise and lived experience that makes this book a trusted, empowering companion for any family beginning their Montessori homeschooling journey."

—Lucie Brixi Tamasova
Founder of Childhood Potential

"As a mom of two preparing to homeschool without any formal training, *The Montessori Homeschooler* gave me the clarity, encouragement, and practical tools I didn't know I needed. Lynda's decades of experience—as both an educator and homeschooling parent—shine through every page, and her voice, which has already inspired me so deeply through social media, felt like a steady hand guiding me with confidence and compassion."

—Yamel Ramos
Creator of @OurMontessoriJourney

"This is the thoughtful and indispensable guide homeschooling families deserve to unlock a child's potential beyond lesson planning—expertly illuminating the true principles of the Montessori philosophy that nurture the whole child, and the sustainable tools to bring it all to life within the home."

—Blanca Velázquez-Martin, MA, LPC
Founder of Whole Child Home

"As one of the world's largest and fastest-growing alternative education paths, there's plenty out there about what Montessori looks like in theory— but far less about how it should feel in practice. Lynda has created a guide for parents that is both practical and rigorous, connecting you to the why— not just the what. You'll still learn how, but in a way that reignites your own relationship to learning, offering a far more sustainable foundation. While most homeschooling resources focus on checklists, printables and lesson plans, this book flips the script and gives voice to the deeper mental, social, emotional, and even spiritual reframing that must come first."

—Jenna Wawrzyniec
Child Development Writer and
Founder of Holding Space Montessori

"Right from the get-go, this book provides clarity on what true Montessori is as a homeschooling method and what focus a Montessori homeschooler should have to authentically implement the scientific pedagogy that has revolutionized education for over a century. Lynda has written a myth-busting, profound, and empowering guide to support home educators in their Montessori journeys."

—Jovis San Diego
Creator of Hometessori

"*The Montessori Homeschooler* is a practical and inspiring deep-dive into the Montessori homeschooling world. Drawing from her years of experience as a trusted Montessori homeschooling coach, Lynda offers new parents the perfect starting point to confidently begin their homeschooling journey."

—Bianca A. Solorzano, M.Ed.
Host of the Montessori Babies Podcast

"I've worked in Montessori classrooms for years, but homeschooling felt like a whole different world. After reading this book, I feel so much more confident and clear about how to support my children at home. Lynda's expertise in Montessori homeschooling was exactly what I needed."

—Kermichelle Leo-Joseph
Creator of @MontessoriInColor and
Founder of Juniper Rose Microschool

"This book is the perfect piece that guides a Montessorian or the average parent who is looking to jump into homeschooling. The Montessori knowledge Lynda has to share along with how to practically homeschool will not only set you and your children up to be successful at homeschooling, but will give you all the confidence you need and help you soar!"

—Rachel Martin
Podcaster and Co-Creator of Montessori Moms in the Wild

The Montessori Homeschooler

A Practical Guide to Get Started with Confidence

Lynda Apostol, M.Ed

JB JOSSEY-BASS™

A Wiley Brand

Published by John Wiley & Sons, Inc., Hoboken, New Jersey.

ISBNs: 9781394281022 (Paperback), 9781394281046 (ePDF), 9781394281039 (ePub).

For general information on our other products and services, please contact our Customer Care Department within the United States at (800) 762-2974, outside the United States at (317) 572-3993. For product technical support, you can find answers to frequently asked questions or reach us via live chat at https://support.wiley.com.

If you believe you've found a mistake in this book, please bring it to our attention by emailing our reader support team at wileysupport@wiley.com with the subject line "Possible Book Errata Submission."

Wiley also publishes its books in a variety of electronic formats. Some content that appears in print may not be available in electronic formats. For more information about Wiley products, visit our website at www.wiley.com.

Library of Congress Cataloging-in-Publication Data is Available

Cover Design: Jon Boylan
Cover Images: © Unchalee Khun/Shutterstock, © ARTpok/Shutterstock
Printed and bound by CPI Group (UK) Ltd, Croydon, CR0 4YY

C9781394281022_041125

To my children, my husband, my mother, and every parent who dared to follow the child—and invited me to guide them along the way.

Contents

Acknowledgments   *xi*

About the Author   *xiii*

Preface   *xv*

Introduction: The Montessori Revolution   *xvii*

SECTION 1   Laying the Groundwork   **1**

Chapter 1   Before You Begin   3

Chapter 2   Breaking Free from the School Mindset   13

Chapter 3   Overcoming Fear and Self-Doubt   23

Chapter 4   Finding Your Why   31

Chapter 5   In It Together   39

SECTION 2   How Montessori Works   **49**

Chapter 6   Montessori vs. Traditional Education   51

Chapter 7   The Three Pillars of Montessori   59

Chapter 8   The Prepared Adult   65

Chapter 9   Freedom Within Limits   71

Chapter 10   Understanding Montessori's Developmental Stages   77

SECTION 3   Bringing It Home   **85**

Chapter 11   The Home That Teaches   87

Chapter 12   The Montessori Learning Space   95

Chapter 13   The Montessori Curriculum for Homeschoolers   105

Chapter 14   Montessori Materials   115

Chapter 15   Creating a Daily Rhythm   125

SECTION 4   From Preparation to Practice   **133**

Chapter 16   Introducing Montessori Lessons   135

Chapter 17   What to Do on Day 1, Week 1, Month 1   145

Chapter 18   Common Roadblocks   153

Chapter 19   Supporting the Whole Child   161

Chapter 20   Observation and Repetition   167

**SECTION 5   Guiding the Montessori
                Learning Experience**   **175**

Chapter 21   Adapting Montessori to Your Family   177

Chapter 22   Fostering Independence Through Practice   185

Chapter 23   Montessori Discipline and Conflict Resolution   193

Chapter 24   Fostering Concentration and Focus   201

Conclusion: What's Next   *209*
Glossary of Montessori Terms   *213*
Appendix: Meet the Montessori Mamas   *221*
Index   *225*

Acknowledgments

Writing this book has been an act of integration—of memory, motherhood, and mission. I could not have done it without the people who grounded me, challenged me, and reminded me why this work matters.

To my children, Kira and Nikko: thank you for being the inspiration and the reason behind everything I do. You've taught me more about trust, patience, and presence than any book ever could.

To my husband, Jason: your unwavering belief in me and in this vision made space for this book to be born. You are my rock—the steady presence through every high, every doubt, and every late-night writing session. Thank you for holding so much so I could create freely. Your presence and support is the throughline in all of it.

To my mother: your strength and sacrifice live in every word I write. You gave me the courage to live my truth and build something different for my family.

To my best friend, Amanda: thank you for standing with me through every season—from classroom days to motherhood to building this work. You've reminded me who I am when I've needed it most. Your friendship has been a mirror, a refuge, and a source of strength every step of the way.

To Susan Fernandez and Paulina Kim—my daughter's early teachers—thank you for welcoming our family with open arms and encouraging me to take a chance on Montessori. Your presence in my daughter's early life became a turning point in mine. This work wouldn't exist without the spark you lit.

To the parents and caregivers—my fellow travelers—who have entrusted me with the honor of guiding their Montessori journey: thank you. You are not my clients. You are the heart of this movement. Your courage to step away from the conventional and walk toward something more intentional is what keeps this work alive.

To my mentors—Phillis Rodgers, Todd Gaviglio, and Elba Maldonado-Colón—thank you for shaping the educator and leader I've become. Your wisdom, guidance, and example have left a lasting imprint on my work and my heart.

To the trainers who built the foundation of my Montessori practice—Dena Stoneman, Debra Sheehan, Sandi Brock, Sara Zamora, and Heather Quantrell—thank you for passing on the depth and dignity of this work with integrity and care.

To the colleagues who have influenced my path and continue to inspire me with their leadership, insight, and dedication—Lia Rosen, Alessandra Pagone Abel, Jared Woods, Lo Howard, and Ashley Ware—thank you for modeling what it means to be both visionary and grounded in service.

To the Montessori community: thank you for holding space for those of us building this work beyond the classroom walls. Your legacy continues in every home transformed with intention and love.

To the Jossey-Bass/Wiley editorial team—Sam Ofman, Navin Vijayakumar, and Kezia Endsley—thank you for championing this vision with clarity, care, and deep respect for both the message and the audience. Your partnership brought this book to life with intention and integrity, and I'm so grateful to have created alongside you.

About the Author

Lynda Apostol, M.Ed., is a Montessori and education specialist with nearly 20 years of experience across public, private, charter, and home-based learning. She's the founder of *The Montessori Teacher LLC* and *The Montessori Homeschool Academy* and a veteran homeschooler. Known for bridging traditional education with authentic Montessori practice, Lynda helps families and educators make confident, child-centered shifts in how they teach and learn. Through her work with homeschoolers, microschools, and learning collectives, she brings clarity, confidence, and real-world strategies to the home education space.

Preface

Dear Reader,

Thank you for picking up this book. Whether you're stepping into Montessori homeschooling with excitement, hesitation, or a thousand unanswered questions, you're in the right place.

This isn't just a book of checklists, activity ideas, or tips and tricks. It's a guide to getting started—with integrity, with confidence, and with clarity. Montessori is a rich, nuanced method that often gets oversimplified or misrepresented, especially in the homeschool world. My goal is to help you cut through the noise and to root yourself in something deeper: the real thing.

I wrote this book because I've seen too many parents try to piece together their homeschool using scattered resources, blog posts, commercialized kits, false claims of authenticity, or watered-down interpretations of Montessori that leave them feeling comforted yet somehow still second-guessing their instincts and doubting their ability to "do it right." I've seen the overwhelm. I've seen the self-doubt. And I've also seen what happens when a parent finally finds solid ground—a clear understanding of the philosophy, reliable guidance, and the confidence to live it out in their own home.

This book is written for you, the parent who is ready to challenge the status quo and claim Montessori with high fidelity to its principles. I'm here to offer you a clear, undiluted foundation—one that respects the intelligence, responsibility, and commitment you bring to this journey. You deserve more than vague inspiration or surface-level advice. You deserve support that honors the depth of your role and the potential of your child.

While the core principles in this book apply across the Montessori journey, the practical tools and examples—especially in Section 4—are designed for children ages 3–9. If you're beginning Montessori with an older child (ages 9+), know that you can still apply this method, but your implementation may look different. Around age 9, children shift from learning to read to reading to learn. At that stage, Montessori becomes more collaborative, research-based, and internally driven. You may find yourself blending Montessori with other methods—and that's okay. With a strong foundation and a flexible mindset, you can create something authentic and developmentally aligned.

Montessori homeschooling doesn't need to feel like a compromise. It doesn't need to imitate a classroom or mimic an Instagram reel. It can be powerful, transformative, and entirely yours. When done with care and integrity, Montessori homeschooling becomes not just an educational method—but a way of living and learning together that nurtures both the child and the adult.

I come to you as both a parent and a professional, with nearly 20 years of experience in public, private, and Montessori education. I've been a teacher, an administrator, a coach, and most importantly, a guide in my own home. I know what it's like to feel unsure. I know the weight of wanting to "get it right." And I know the transformation that happens when we stop chasing perfection and start building trust—in the method, in our children, and in ourselves.

This book doesn't give you a step-by-step script or a plug-and-play curriculum. Instead, it gives you what you actually need to begin: a strong foundation, a thoughtful framework, and the tools to adapt Montessori to your real life—without diluting the method or losing your way.

I hope this book feels like a trusted friend—here to empower, challenge, and walk with you as you bring Montessori into your home. My goal is for you to close this book with more confidence in yourself, more clarity in your role as a guide, and a renewed sense of possibility for your child's education.

This is just the beginning—and you are more ready than you think.

With deep respect and unwavering belief in your journey,

Lynda Apostol, M.Ed

Introduction: The Montessori Revolution

Why We Need a New Model and How to Build It at Home

You're here because you believe education should be more than worksheets, test scores, and rigid curricula. You're here because something inside you knows—learning should be deeper, richer, more meaningful.

Maybe you're frustrated with traditional models that stifle curiosity and replace joy with compliance. Maybe you've been told you need to settle for a watered-down version of Montessori—because homeschooling "can't be the real thing." Or maybe you're just plain overwhelmed, trying to piece together what Montessori homeschooling should look like while second-guessing every decision along the way.

Let me be clear: *Montessori homeschooling is not a compromise. It's an opportunity.*

Education at home isn't a substitute for school—it's a *different paradigm entirely.*

The goal isn't to replicate the classroom. It's to create something better. Something that honors your child's natural development. Something that respects their independence, invites their curiosity, and supports their growth into confident, capable, self-directed learners. Something that aligns not only with *who your child is*, but with the values that matter to your family.

And yes—you can do this.

Montessori isn't reserved for trained teachers in pristine classrooms inside of well-funded schools. It's not about being perfect. It doesn't require an endless supply of expensive materials or a rigid script to follow.

It's a method—a time-tested, research-backed approach to human development that you, as a homeschooling parent, *can learn, internalize, and live*. Not just as a method of education but as a philosophy for life.

This book isn't about idealized versions of Montessori that only work in carefully controlled environments. It's about *real* Montessori home-schooling: Practical. Grounded. Rooted in human development. Adapted for home. Built around *your* real life. I'll give you the tools, the knowledge, and the confidence to build a truly authentic Montessori homeschool—without the fluff, the oversimplification, or the limiting beliefs that say, "this isn't possible outside a classroom."

You don't have to settle for a surface-level, "Montessori-inspired" experience that compromises the integrity of the method. You don't have to patch together advice from strangers on the internet who may not fully understand the philosophy themselves.

You deserve the real thing. And more importantly—your child does, too.

What This Book Will Teach You

Let's begin with a simple truth: *Montessori homeschooling is a journey, not a checklist.*

This book isn't about memorizing lesson scripts or creating the perfect shelf display. It's about who you become—not just what you do. It's about learning to see your child with new eyes, to trust the process, and to lead with purpose and presence.

You won't find a one-size-fits-all curriculum or a rigid "how-to" formula in these pages. Instead, you'll be invited to think like a Montessorian, to approach life at home through the lens of observation, respect, and growth.

This book guides you in preparing your mindset, your environment, and your rhythm—so you can support your child with clarity and confidence.

You'll learn:

- How to prepare yourself as the Montessori guide in your home. (Hint: Montessori begins with you, not your child.)
- How to design a home environment that fosters independence, curiosity, and deep engagement—*without needing a classroom's worth of materials.*
- How to understand Montessori's approach across the full spectrum—from practical life to academic subjects—so you can introduce lessons with ease and meaning.
- How to create a daily rhythm that balances structure and flexibility, allowing learning to unfold naturally while honoring your child's developmental needs.
- How to discern what materials actually serve your child's growth—and how to avoid wasting money on things that don't.
- How to embrace Montessori homeschooling as a lifestyle—not a trend, not a temporary fix, but a deeply aligned way of raising and educating your child at home.

You'll also find a glossary of key terms at the end of the book. If you're new to this world, don't worry—I've defined many of the concepts and vocabulary you'll encounter so you can follow along with clarity and confidence.

But this book isn't just information—it's the beginning of your transformation.

Throughout the chapters, you'll meet real families from all walks of life who are living this journey. Their stories—woven throughout—offer perspective, honesty, and inspiration.

You'll also find a companion reflection and implementation journal to help you apply what you're learning right away. These prompts are designed to deepen your self-awareness—because in Montessori, preparedness begins with the adult.

This book meets you where you are, whether you're just starting out or shifting gears. Step by step, we'll walk together toward a Montessori homeschool life that is grounded, thoughtful, and completely doable.

Why Montessori? Why Now?

More families than ever before are stepping outside the traditional education system—seeking something deeper, something more aligned with how children actually grow and learn. They're reclaiming the freedom to educate their children in ways that honor both development and dignity.

Montessori homeschooling isn't just an alternative. It's a quiet revolution.

A revolution against the idea that children must be controlled. Against the assumption that learning must be standardized. Against the belief that only "experts" are qualified to guide a child's education.

Montessori invites us to see education differently.

Education is not something *done* to the child. It is a process of supporting what is already unfolding within them. Learning emerges from within the child—when they're offered the right environment, the right tools, and the right kind of guidance.

Montessori offers a balanced approach. Rooted in freedom and responsibility. Driven by curiosity and structure. Grounded in respect for the child—without abandoning clarity, sequence, or accountability.

This is not rigid "school-at-home," nor is it a free-for-all. It is a thoughtful, intentional method that supports your child's natural development—while ensuring they gain the skills, knowledge, and habits of mind they need to thrive in the real world.

And you?

You are part of this movement.

By choosing Montessori homeschooling, you are choosing to trust your child. To trust yourself. And to trust a method that has transformed education across cultures and continents for more than a century.

This book helps you take that trust—and turn it into meaningful action.

You don't have to settle for less. You don't have to rely on social media scraps or prepackaged curriculums that dilute the philosophy. You don't need to wait until you feel "fully ready." You're ready now.

You are capable of giving your child an authentic Montessori education at home.

And it all starts here.

Let's begin.

Laying the Groundwork

Clarifying Your Purpose, Preparing Your Home, and Reimagining Education

Before you can confidently guide your child, you have to ground yourself— *not* in a curriculum, but in clarity, courage, and connection.

This first section is where that grounding begins.

You might be feeling excited. You might be feeling overwhelmed. You've chosen a path that goes against the grain—and that takes real intention. Montessori homeschooling is not about replicating school at home or rushing into materials and routines. It's about transformation—from the inside out.

This section is designed to help you build a strong inner framework before you ever step into a lesson. Because before your child begins their Montessori journey, *you* begin yours.

In the chapters ahead, you explore what Montessori homeschooling really is (and isn't), how to break free from old school mindsets, and how to face the doubts and fears that inevitably arise when you step into something new. You'll reflect on your deeper motivations and begin to define your "why." And you'll start to think about what it means to build a home culture that truly supports this work—not just academically, but emotionally and relationally.

By the time you finish this section, you'll feel more aligned, more clear, and more equipped to lead your homeschool—not from a place of pressure, but from a place of purpose.

This is the groundwork. This is where your journey truly begins.

Let's begin together.

1

Before You Begin

What Montessori Homeschooling Is and When It Starts

When to Homeschool: Understanding Montessori's Developmental Timing

One of the most common questions families ask is, "When should we start homeschooling?"

If you've spent any time in online communities or researching curriculum options, you've probably noticed that many approaches to homeschooling begin around kindergarten or first grade. Montessori is different.

In Montessori, homeschooling typically begins at age 3—not because we're pushing academics early, but because this is when a major shift occurs in your child's development. Around this age, your child enters the second half of what we call the *first plane of development* (ages 0–6). This is when they begin transitioning from unconscious absorption to conscious learning.

That's a big deal.

In the first 3 years of life, your child learns effortlessly through *unconscious absorption*. Their brain is like a sponge, soaking in language, movement,

3

order, and relationships simply through experience. This is not the time for formal academics—but it *is* the time to lay the essential groundwork that academic learning depends on later.

Through practical life activities, sensory exploration, language-rich interactions (think narration, think-alouds, reading every night), family connection and the freedom to move and concentrate, your infant and toddler is developing the foundations of what Montessori calls the *mathematical mind,* the *coordinated hand,* and the *ordered intellect.* These aren't buzzwords—they're real, observable capacities that emerge through rich and respectful environments.

So while this book doesn't focus on Montessori at home in the 0–3 stage, it's important to acknowledge how vital those early years are. We are *laying the foundation for a lifetime of learning*—even if that learning doesn't look like "school."

Homeschooling, or formal education and academic instruction, in the Montessori context begins in earnest at age three, when your child becomes developmentally ready for more intentional, structured guidance—but always in harmony with their natural rhythms and readiness. It's not school-at-home, and it's not early push-down academics. It's a child-led, adult-supported approach that respects the absorbent mind while offering carefully sequenced, hands-on learning experiences.

This is also the age when the Montessori materials start to shine. The sandpaper letters, number rods, sound games, and golden beads weren't designed for older children—they were created precisely for the sensitive periods that begin around age three. It's when the child is ready to move from absorbing the world around them to actively engaging with it in purposeful ways.

So if you're wondering *why* Montessori and *why now*, it's because Montessori aligns with your child's natural developmental timeline—not with arbitrary school start dates.

We begin homeschooling at age three not to get ahead, but to meet the child *right where they are.*

> "Montessori doesn't begin with school—it begins with life. But formal homeschooling begins when your child is ready to *consciously* engage with learning—and that's around age three."

What Is Montessori Homeschooling?

The following two terms are often used interchangeably by parents and educators alike—but they're not quite the same and it's important to understand this distinction:

- **Montessori at home** refers to applying Montessori principles to daily life and parenting—things like offering choices within limits, preparing a child-accessible environment, using respectful language, and encouraging independence in daily routines. This approach starts from birth and extends throughout childhood, regardless of whether formal homeschooling is taking place.
- **Montessori homeschooling**, by contrast, begins when the child is developmentally ready for conscious learning—typically around age three. It involves a more intentional educational rhythm, the use of Montessori materials and lesson sequences, and a home environment specifically prepared for academic engagement. It is not just parenting with Montessori values; it is guiding your child's education in alignment with the Montessori method.

In short:

- **Montessori at home** = Lifestyle and parenting philosophy
- **Montessori homeschooling** = Educational method and academic rhythm

Both are valuable. But this book focuses on the second: how to begin your journey to bringing authentic Montessori education into your home with clarity, confidence, and developmental integrity.

To support you in this journey, I explore the core Montessori values that guide this approach—principles like respect for the child, independence, freedom within limits, observation, and the prepared environment. These values shape not just what you do, but how and why you do it. You'll encounter them throughout this book, and if you're new to Montessori, you may want to refer to the glossary at the end for clear definitions and explanation of key terms.

The Core Values Behind Montessori

Montessori isn't just a set of materials or a sequence of lessons—it's a philosophy guided by deeply held values that shape how we see the child and how we support their development. These principles are what make Montessori truly transformative, and they're just as powerful at home as they are in a classroom.

Some of the key values you'll encounter throughout this book include:

- **Respect for the child:** Seeing the child as a whole, capable human being with agency, preferences, and potential, not an empty vessel to be filled.
- **Independence:** Trusting the child's capabilities and creating opportunities for the child to do things themselves, building confidence and real-world competence.
- **Freedom within limits:** Allowing meaningful choice and autonomy while maintaining boundaries that ensure safety, order, and respect for others.
- **Prepared environment:** Intentionally designing the child's space and curating the objects and materials within it to invite exploration, concentration, and meaningful work.
- **Observation:** Watching closely (without hovering) to learn, not to assess or control, so you can understand what the child needs, when they're ready, and how to support them effectively.
- **Follow the child:** Understanding the child's stages of development and their motivations for work to respond to their inner drive by working in collaboration with their natural rhythms, interests, and readiness to guide the learning process.

These values are more than concepts—they're practices. You'll see them woven into the structure of this book and tools I share and in the stories from real Montessori families.

If you're unfamiliar with the terminology, don't worry. There's a glossary at the end of the book with many of the key terms and concepts you'll encounter as you read. You don't need to memorize them up front—just know that support is there when you need it.

Why Families Choose to Homeschool

Homeschooling is a deeply personal decision, and families arrive at it for all kinds of reasons. Maybe you're here because you want more time with your child, or because you feel traditional schools aren't meeting their needs. Maybe you love the idea of tailoring education to your child's unique learning style. Or maybe you've just always felt called to something different.

For many families, homeschooling is about *freedom*—freedom to move at a child's pace, to explore topics deeply, to nurture creativity, and to spend quality time together as a family. Homeschooling is a vehicle that helps you create a learning environment that aligns with your values, rather than fitting into a one-size-fits-all system.

I remember when I first started considering homeschooling. I kept thinking, *Can I really do this? Am I going to mess this up?* The self-doubt was real. But when I took a step back and asked myself what I truly wanted for my child—joyful learning, curiosity, independence, meaningful experiences, belonging—I realized that no one was better equipped to provide that than me. If you're feeling that same hesitation, know this: homeschooling isn't about having all the answers, being a subject-matter expert, or being able to control the future. It's about presence, intention, self-discipline, and a willingness to learn alongside your child.

The Appeal of Montessori Homeschooling

Montessori offers something rare: a method that respects the whole child while providing a clear framework for academic development. It is both structured and flexible, grounded in developmental science yet adaptable to your home.

If you've seen Montessori mentioned online—in blog posts, parenting groups, or on social media—you may have noticed the focus on clean spaces, minimalist shelves, and curated wooden materials. Maybe you've wondered, *Is this something I can actually do at home?*

The answer is: yes. But not because you can replicate a classroom. Because your home is already rich with potential.

And while many are first drawn to Montessori because of its aesthetic, Montessori isn't about matching a look or collecting the right materials—it's about cultivating the conditions for deep, meaningful learning. It's a method—a mindset—and a skillset. It's about learning how to prepare developmentally informed environments for both living and learning and about preparing *yourself* so your child can engage, explore, and grow within them.

Unlike traditional homeschooling methods, which often center on textbooks, step-by-step curricula, and adult-led instruction, Montessori does not rely on workbooks or top-down instruction. Instead, it invites the child to explore materials with intrinsic control of error, to follow their interests within a prepared environment, and to develop independence in both thought and action. Your role is not to deliver lessons on command, but to prepare the environment, observe, and offer the right lesson at the right time.

Children don't build themselves from nothing—they build themselves through experience. Through exploration. Through meaningful work. Montessori provides a framework for self-construction—and when adapted thoughtfully to the home, it becomes not just possible but powerful.

Montessori works beautifully in a homeschool setting because:

- It naturally integrates with real life—cooking, cleaning, gardening, shopping, budgeting
- It values uninterrupted work periods and deep concentration
- It allows for personalization and self-paced learning
- It positions the adult as a guide, not a gatekeeper

When done authentically, Montessori homeschooling strengthens family connections, builds mutual respect, and cultivates lifelong learners.

The Benefits of Montessori in a Homeschool Setting

When you bring Montessori into your home, you're not just teaching your child—you're transforming the way your family learns and interacts. Here's why this approach is so rewarding:

- **Individualized and personalized learning:** Your child learns at their own pace in line with their development in meaningful ways. It's about guiding your child to become their best selves, to find their purpose in the world—not about pressure to meet arbitrary benchmarks.

- **Real-life integration:** Montessori is designed for real-world learning. Everyday life—cooking, gardening, tidying, grocery shopping, budgeting, self-care—becomes part of your child's education, not just hypothetically but in actuality.
- **Stronger parent–child connection:** Homeschooling gives you the chance to truly *see* your child—to understand how they learn, what excites them, and what challenges them. More than anything, homeschooling is about togetherness and prioritizing what matters most.
- **A love for learning:** Montessori fosters deep curiosity, exploration, and a lifelong love of discovery. You get to nurture your own love of learning, and in doing so, you foster theirs.

Why Families Struggle to Bring Montessori Home

Many families struggle to implement Montessori at home not because they lack dedication—but because they begin in the wrong place.

They often:

- Start with materials and lessons before preparing themselves or the environment.
- Confuse inspiration with implementation.
- Personalize the philosophy to themselves instead of the child.

You might find yourself researching lessons for a three-year-old before you've taken time to observe their interests. Or maybe you bought all the wooden toys and baskets, but the day still feels chaotic and disconnected.

That's because the core of Montessori isn't about the stuff—it's about the prepared adult and the intentional environment.

> "Montessori is personalized—but it's personalized to the child, not the adult."

If you're looking for ease and convenience for the adult, Montessori might not be the right fit. But if you're looking to honor who your child truly is, you're in the right place.

What Comes Next

By now, you understand that Montessori homeschooling doesn't begin with a boxed curriculum, a checklist, or a shelf full of materials. It begins with *a shift in perspective*.

You're stepping into a new rhythm—one that's guided by development, grounded in trust, and powered by presence. That shift doesn't require you to have all the answers right now. It simply asks you to stay curious, stay humble, and stay committed to your child's unfolding.

As we move forward, we're going to talk about the biggest obstacle most new homeschoolers face—not the materials, not the schedule, not the self-doubt. . . but the mindset they're still carrying from their own schooling.

In the next chapter, you explore what it means to break free from the school mindset, so you can build something better—not just for your child, but for yourself.

You're not just doing school differently. You're doing learning differently. And it starts by seeing it through a new lens.

Let's begin there.

Thoughts from the Frontlines

How real parents made the leap into Montessori homeschooling and what helped them move from uncertainty to intention.

Destiny: Single mom, global lens, African diaspora

"I began homeschooling when my son was two years and nine months. It has been the most challenging thing—beside childbirth, ha—that I have ever done, and by far, the most gratifying. What I love the most is the constant challenge. Whether it's watching him make connections on his own, or the way this has pushed me to grow and heal myself, it's already been such a gift."

Maria Isabel: Trilingual family living in Sweden

"I live in Sweden with my husband and our four and a half-year-old son. We speak Spanish, English, and Swedish in our home. I started homeschooling with a DIY mindset—just me, some books, and a lot of improvising. But the more I learned about Montessori, the more I realized how intentional it really is. I couldn't keep winging it. Seeking support was a turning point."

Mae-Lin: Military veteran, trauma-informed journey

"I never thought I'd have a child, and now I can't imagine life without my daughter. I want her to question everything—songs, social norms, religion, power. I want her to be emotionally intelligent, to see conflict as normal, to feel free to fail. I want her to grow up unafraid. Montessori felt like a method that honored all of that."

Sarah: Mother of four, Montessori-inspired since birth

"We've homeschooled from the beginning. At first, I leaned on what I knew—traditional methods with Montessori on the side. But when I saw how drained we both felt, I knew something had to change. Montessori gave us back the joy. It gave me a way to meet my kids where they are instead of where the curriculum said they should be."

Tiffany: Colombian-American, homeschooling in Spanish

"I don't have a background in education, and I'm homeschooling my girls in Spanish while learning other languages together. It's not always easy, but it's deeply meaningful. Montessori matched everything I was already feeling and doing intuitively. Even when we tried a Montessori school, I knew in my gut that I could give my kids something more personal at home."

Wilka: Bilingual working mom, Montessori as mindset

"I thought I was doing Montessori—but I was just checking off boxes. It wasn't until I found a better guide that I realized this is about mindset. Montessori taught me to slow down, to observe, to trust the child. And it taught me that I don't need to be the one with all the answers. I just need to be willing to grow alongside her."

Wennie: Nurse, homeschooling in a small apartment

"We live in a small space and I work part-time, so Montessori homeschooling felt almost impossible at first. There were so many materials, so many subjects. I was overwhelmed. But I knew I couldn't afford to do this halfway. I didn't want to risk my child's education. Once I committed to being the prepared adult, everything began to shift."

To learn more about the families featured throughout this book, you'll find their bios in the appendix.

2

Breaking Free from the School Mindset

Understanding Deschooling and Unlearning Old Paradigms

If you've spent any time researching homeschooling, you've probably come across the term *deschooling*. Maybe you've read—or gotten the impression—that it simply means taking a break from academics after leaving traditional school. Or that it's just a season of letting kids "just be" to reconnect and unwind. There's a grain of truth in those ideas. But the real heart of deschooling goes much deeper.

Deschooling isn't just a break from school. It's the intentional process of unlearning deeply ingrained beliefs about education—beliefs that often continue to shape the way you think learning *should* look, even when they no longer serve you or your children.

You may have chosen to step away from the classroom. But if you're still measuring success through outcomes, looking for step-by-step curriculum scripts, or structuring your day around what *you* need to deliver rather than what your child is ready for—then chances are, the traditional schooling paradigm is still living in your mind and habits.

Montessori homeschooling cannot thrive within that framework. And yet, many creators and companies try to make it fit—standardizing lessons, building open-and-go plans, or selling comfort disguised as Montessori.

Familiar? Yes.

Transformative? Not even close.

Montessori is not a rebranding of school. It's a reimagining of education itself. It is an entirely different way of understanding how children learn, one that requires parents and educators to shift their mindset first. It challenges you to think differently, observe more carefully, and let go of what no longer serves your children or yourself.

In this chapter, you explore what deschooling really means, why it's essential before fully implementing Montessori at home, and how to begin unlearning outdated paradigms so you can build something better.

Why Do You Need to Deschool?

Imagine you've spent years driving on the right side of the road. One day, you move to a country where people drive on the left. Even though you understand the rule change, your instincts fight it. You reach for the wrong side of the car, hesitate at intersections, and feel an overwhelming sense of disorientation and perhaps a tinge of fear. You have to actively grow your awareness so you can consciously make intentional choices so you can relearn and break the old habit you once had set to autopilot.

That's what shifting from traditional education to Montessori home-schooling feels like.

You *know* this is different. You want to embrace it. You want to do it differently. But unless you intentionally retrain your perspective, you'll default to old patterns and traditional schooling mindset traps—adult-led lessons, boxed curriculum, performance-based assessment, perfectionism, self-doubt when you don't get it right the first time—or the opposite extreme—living in echo chambers that encourage you to give up all structure and hope it all works itself out.

You may find yourself asking, "What should I be teaching today?" and feeling relief when a curriculum hands you a checklist. Or you may catch yourself getting anxious if your child isn't producing a tangible result—like a finished worksheet, a craft, or a reading milestone—wondering if learning is really happening. You may cling to a scripted plan that promises outcomes, just to feel like you're on solid ground.

And when that plan doesn't deliver? You might swing in the other direction—telling yourself you're "just following the child" while secretly worrying when their interest fizzles or doesn't lead to something you can measure. You might even feel guilty or inadequate for not being able to replicate what you see other homeschoolers doing online.

These are the moments when the old paradigm sneaks back in—not because you believe in it, but because it feels safer than the unknown.

Deschooling Helps You Rebuild from the Ground Up

Deschooling takes time. It doesn't begin when you leave traditional school. It begins when you start trying to live and learn in a new way—and bump into all the old thoughts that come with you.

And while, if you're leaving a classroom setting, it may be necessary to take a break to gather your thoughts and get organized when you first get started, it's important to recognize that a break is just that—a break. Deschooling is a process of strengthening self-awareness that makes way for the transformation to come, not a pause before returning to business as usual.

What Deschooling Is and Isn't

Many parents assume deschooling means "doing nothing." No plans, no materials, no routine—just letting kids be. But Montessori families know better.

Deschooling is an *active* process. It's about:

- Observing your child without judgment or intervention
- Releasing the belief that learning must look a certain way
- Rebuilding trust in your child's natural desire to learn
- Reframing education from something delivered to something discovered

This kind of work requires intention. It's not about throwing out structure but about replacing outdated models with ones that support authentic growth.

Why Traditional Models Are Hard to Let Go

Let's be honest—traditional schooling is familiar. And in times of uncertainty, the familiar feels safe.

Homeschooling—especially in the beginning—can feel like standing at the edge of a cliff. You're stepping into something new without a road map. And when that discomfort hits, it's only natural to reach for what you know, even when it no longer serves you: schedules, checklists, workbooks, and sequenced, all-in-one curriculum guides that promise to do the thinking for you.

But the truth is, those tools often reinforce the very mindset you're trying to leave behind.

Even trained Montessori educators can fall back into traditional habits when doubt creeps in. As Angeline Stoll Lillard writes in *Montessori: The Science Behind the Genius*:

> "Traditional teaching fits both a teacher's memory and the culturally dominant view of what school is, and teachers who have less understanding of alternatives will naturally fall back on it."[1]

The same goes for homeschooling parents. We may begin with Montessori ideals, but when we get anxious, we often revert—defaulting to old ways of teaching because they feel more concrete than trusting the child's process.

This is why deschooling is *non-negotiable*. Without it, you risk re-creating school-at-home instead of truly transforming your approach to education and building a home where learning can unfold to support your children in reaching their true potential.

Why Paradigms Matter

Education is shaped by paradigms—mental models that influence how people view learning, teaching, and progress.

Most of us grew up in a system rooted in traditional, industrial-era schooling. This model is built on the idea that children are passive recipients of knowledge. That learning must be standardized. That performance matters more than process.

Even when we consciously reject traditional schooling, those beliefs often linger beneath the surface—shaping how we show up as educators, especially in moments of uncertainty or when our child wants to learn something new. We may say we've stepped away from the old system, but our instincts still reach for its tools and templates when the pressure is on.

For example:

- Worrying if your child isn't reading by a certain age? That's a traditional paradigm.
- Needing a worksheet to feel like learning happened? Traditional paradigm.
- Believing you must *know* every subject in depth before you can guide your child through it? Traditional paradigm.
- Expecting learning to happen in packaged lessons you can check off sequentially? Traditional paradigm.
- Measuring success by output (how much work gets done) instead of engagement? Traditional paradigm.

The Montessori Paradigm

Montessori asks something radical: to release those beliefs and flip those assumptions on their head.

- Instead of age-based benchmarks dictated by politically motivated standards, we observe each child's unique developmental path and guide them toward real developmental milestones.
- Instead of assessing through worksheets and tests, we rely on scientific observation of the child's engagement in hands-on, purposeful activity.
- Instead of seeing our role as the keeper of knowledge—or relying on entertainment to manipulate the child into learning what we want them to learn—we become facilitators of learning experiences and offer meaningful, real-life work that satisfies the child's need for purpose and contribution.

- Instead of enforcing compliance, we guide the child toward internal self-regulation and personal responsibility.
- Instead of rigid, sequential lessons, we follow a carefully prepared, flexible progression that breaks down isolated skills and builds the child's ability to become a self-directed learner.

Shifting out of the traditional schooling paradigm isn't just about changing what you teach—it's about changing how you *think* about education altogether. Montessori educates to the child's potential by developing skillsets, critical thinking, and self-discipline. You cannot limit their potential with your own limited knowledge. If you're doing your job well, they should surpass you.

"Your task isn't to know everything—it's to equip them with the tools to learn anything."

Authentic Montessori isn't about prettier materials, themed units, or child-led chaos. It's not an open-and-go solution because it can't be standardized. It's a system of education that's deeply intentional, rooted in child development, driven by observation, and genuinely transformative. It challenges everything you thought you knew about teaching and learning—it doesn't simply validate it.

Deschooling helps you begin this shift—from managing a student to supporting a learner. It's not just about removing old habits. It's about building a new foundation for how you think about learning, growth, and the role of the adult in the process.

How to Begin Deschooling (For Yourself and Your Child)

You won't "arrive" at a deschooled mindset overnight. But this section explains how you can begin the transformation.

Observe Before You Act

Take a step back and watch your child. Without correcting, steering, or prompting. Just observe. What do they gravitate toward? How do they solve problems? Where do they get stuck? This is the first step to understanding how they learn—and it will inform everything you do.

Shift from Teaching to Facilitating

Instead of asking, "What do I need to teach today?" shift to "What kind of environment would invite engagement and discovery?" Montessori learning doesn't happen because you deliver a flawless lesson. It happens because the environment speaks to the child—and you've learned to trust that conversation.

Let Go of Immediate Results

Deschooling requires patience. You may not see clear academic progress right away, and that's okay. Traditional schooling taught us to expect quick proof of progress. Montessori is slower, deeper, and rooted in process over product. Trust that real learning is happening—even if you can't measure it yet.

Examine Your Own Beliefs

Ask:

- What do I believe about how children learn?
- Where did those beliefs come from?
- Are they rooted in fear or trust?

Deschooling starts with self-awareness. You can't teach differently if you're still thinking the same.

Create a Prepared Environment

Montessori isn't about having the "right" materials—it's about having the right conditions. Section 3: Bringing It Home, digs into the prepared environment in detail. But for now, focus on simplifying your learning space, decluttering your home, and observing how your child uses what's available.

Trust the Process

This work is slow and sacred. It doesn't produce instant validation—but it cultivates something much more powerful: self-motivated, curious, capable learners. And yes—that begins with you.

What Comes Next

Deschooling is not a season of nothingness. It's the first step in becoming the prepared adult.

The more you clarify your mindset, the less you'll scramble for materials, cling to control, or measure your worth by your child's output. Montessori becomes sustainable not because you're doing more, but because you're thinking differently.

This isn't about throwing away structure. It's about exchanging outdated ideas for something richer, more humane, and far more aligned with how children actually grow.

The path to authentic Montessori homeschooling doesn't start with a lesson plan. It starts with you.

And this is where your real transformation begins.

Thoughts from the Frontlines

Reflections on letting go of perfectionism, control, and traditional schooling beliefs to embrace a more intuitive, responsive way of learning.

Mae-Lin: Veteran, recovering perfectionist

"I had analysis paralysis. I kept rewatching the same course videos, thinking I had to understand it *all* before I could begin. I was so afraid of doing it wrong. I didn't realize I was still thinking like a traditional student—waiting to be 'ready' before I could try. Healing my nervous system helped me finally move forward. I had to learn to just start."

Wilka: Multicultural mom, former checklist thinker

"I came into Montessori with the mindset that I had to 'teach' everything and check it off. But that wasn't it. I realized I was still holding onto the idea that I had to be the keeper of knowledge. Montessori shifted that. Now I know it's not about having all the answers—it's about watching, listening, and preparing the environment so the learning can emerge."

Fatema: Stay-at-home mom in Saudi Arabia, overcoming self-doubt

"I felt like I was my biggest obstacle. I've always struggled with consistency and discipline, and I didn't know if I could stick with it. But when I looked at the kind of childhood I wanted for my kids, I knew I had to break the cycle and try something different. That's what gave me the push to finally begin."

Sarah: Mom of four, letting go of traditional timelines

"When I first started homeschooling, I was afraid my kids wouldn't 'keep up' with public school. I clung to traditional curriculum as a safety net. But it drained the joy out of learning. Once I let that go and trusted Montessori's developmental pace, everything changed. They started learning because they *wanted* to."

Tiffany: First-generation homeschooler, embracing flexibility

"I used to get overwhelmed because I didn't know what the 'right way' to homeschool looked like. I kept searching for examples, for someone to show me exactly how it should be done. But what I really needed was clarity about our values. Once I had that, I could let go of comparison and just focus on building something that worked for *us*."

Viviana: Small business owner, shifting control

"When my daughter started virtual school, I realized how much she was waiting to be told what to do. She had learned to be passive. Transitioning to Montessori made me realize how much control traditional schooling had over our minds—mine included. It took time, but I started watching her make her own choices, and I knew we were finally on the right path."

To learn more about the families featured throughout this book, you'll find their bios in the appendix.

Note

1. Lillard, Angeline Stoll, *Montessori: The Science Behind the Genius* (Oxford University Press, 2005).

3

Overcoming Fear and Self-Doubt

Stepping into Your Role as a Montessori Educator

Starting your Montessori homeschooling journey is exciting—but let's be honest, it can also feel vulnerable. The moment you decide to take ownership of your child's education, all kinds of fears can surface:

Am I qualified? Can I really do this? What if I fail my child?

If you've asked yourself those questions, you're not alone. And more importantly, it means you care. Deeply. That care is not a weakness—it's your strength. But caring doesn't always come with clarity, especially when you're stepping into something unfamiliar.

Most of us were raised to believe that education is something delivered by an expert—someone with credentials, authority, and a classroom. So it's only natural to second-guess yourself when you step into this new role without those external validations. And with the overwhelming amount of Montessori information online—some helpful, some contradictory—it's easy to fall into a spiral of hesitation and self-doubt.

But here's what I want you to remember: Growth isn't supposed to feel comfortable. It stretches you. The doubts you're feeling aren't signs you're on the wrong path—they're evidence that you're on the cusp of transformation.

This chapter helps you unpack your fears, reframe them, and move forward with a little more courage and a lot more clarity. Together, we'll explore some of the most common worries new Montessori homeschoolers face— from qualifications and socialization to academics and outside judgment—so you can step into this work with grounded confidence and a sense of purpose.

Am I Qualified to Teach My Child?

One of the most common fears for new Montessori homeschoolers is the worry that they're not "qualified" to teach. Without a teaching degree or formal Montessori certification, it's easy to feel like you're somehow not enough. But let's take a step back and look at what truly qualifies someone to guide a child.

Montessori education isn't about playing the part of the perfect teacher. It's not about delivering information or controlling outcomes. It's about observing, connecting, and creating an environment that supports growth. And who better to do that than someone who already knows your child deeply, sees their quirks and strengths, and is committed to their long-term development?

Dr. Maria Montessori often emphasized that what makes a great guide is not credentials—but qualities like patience, humility, and respect for the child. These aren't things you earn through certification. These are the qualities you bring to the table as a parent every day.

Of course, Montessori does require a learning curve. You're not expected to know everything right away. But you are expected to be curious, open, and willing to learn. That's your real qualification. Not a title, not a degree— but a mindset. One that says: *I'm here to observe. I'm here to grow. I'm here to serve.*

Instead of trying to master everything up front, start with the basics: slow down, observe your child, and respond with intention. Ask more questions than you answer. Pay attention to what draws their focus. Create space for discovery—not just theirs, but yours too. Your ability to learn alongside your child will do far more for their education than any pre-planned curriculum ever could.

So, are you "qualified"? Yes—because you are willing. Because you care. Because you're here, doing the work. And that matters more than anything else.

What About Socialization?

Ah yes—the big "S" word. "But what about socialization?"

It's one of the most common questions homeschoolers hear. And when you're just starting out, it's a question that can sneak into your own thoughts, too. After all, most of us grew up believing that school was the only place where children learned how to interact with others.

But Montessori helps reframe that. Socialization isn't about being surrounded by peers all day—it's about learning how to live in community and how to communicate with respect, solve problems, and contribute meaningfully to shared spaces. And that kind of social growth doesn't require a classroom. It requires real-life interaction, mixed-age groups, and opportunities to engage authentically with people of all kinds—not just kids born in the same calendar year.

Montessori homes often offer *more* social diversity than traditional school settings. Your child learns how to speak with adults at the grocery store, cooperate with siblings, help a younger child at co-op, or share responsibilities in your home. These are not lesser forms of socialization—they are richer ones. They're rooted in real life.

Still, it's important to be intentional. As a homeschooler, you *do* need to provide opportunities for connection—but those opportunities don't have to look like recess or lunchtime chatter. Think nature groups, community classes, field trips, art lessons, or even shared chores at home. When your child is involved in meaningful work with others, social skills grow naturally.

What you're building isn't a social life that mimics school—it's a social life that reflects the real world. One where people of different ages, backgrounds, and abilities interact in genuine, respectful ways. And that's not just good enough—it's ideal.

As Brené Brown puts it:

> "Fitting in is about assessing a situation and becoming who you need to be to be accepted. Belonging, on the other hand, doesn't require us to change who we are; it requires us to be who we are."[1]

That's what Montessori is about—belonging, not conformity.

Will My Child Fall Behind?

Behind what? According to whom?

This fear usually arises from internalized timelines—the idea that every child must hit a certain benchmark at a certain age or else they're behind. But Montessori doesn't measure learning in lockstep grade levels. It recognizes that development is non-linear, individualized, and often cyclical.

That said, Montessori does offer a framework for understanding progress—it just looks very different from traditional school standards. Instead of grade levels, it works in terms of planes of development. Children grow through distinct stages, and within each stage (like ages 3–6), there's a wide range of what is considered developmentally appropriate.

Think of it like this: In high school or college, students accumulate credits across several years to earn a degree. Similarly, Montessori looks at multi-year developmental cycles. For example, by the end of the first plane of development (birth to age six), a child will likely reach key milestones in their physical, emotional, social, and intellectual growth. These aren't arbitrary academic benchmarks—they're rooted in human development.

Montessori educators understand that certain milestones—like developing the ability to write—are not themselves developmental milestones but rather human technologies that build on underlying developmental foundations. Writing depends on coordination, fine motor strength, language acquisition, memory, and more. Those foundational developments are what Montessori supports intentionally so that skills like writing can emerge naturally and joyfully when the child is ready.

In other words, Montessori educators align instruction with the child's natural readiness. They don't teach to meet external timelines—they guide to support internal development.

So no, your child isn't falling behind if they don't follow a school's arbitrary calendar. They're moving forward on *their* timeline, building real skills and deeper understanding along the way.

It's not about rushing toward outcomes—it's about nurturing the *process* of learning. That's where real confidence, capability, and competence are born.

How Do I Balance Homeschooling with Everything Else?

You're probably juggling a lot—parenting, household tasks, work, and now education. The key isn't doing *everything*. It's to establish clear priorities.

Homeschooling doesn't happen in a vacuum. You're still parenting, running a household, managing relationships, and maybe even working part- or full-time. It's no wonder many parents wonder, *How am I supposed to do it all?*

The short answer: you're not. Montessori isn't about doing everything—it's about doing the right things with intention and consistency. That starts with understanding that balance doesn't mean equal time and energy poured into every category of life. It means creating rhythms that protect what matters most while giving yourself permission to let go of the rest.

In Montessori, the three-hour work cycle is a core element—not because it's a rigid rule, but because it protects a window of uninterrupted focus. That kind of deep work time helps your child build concentration, independence, and flow. And when it becomes a regular part of your routine, it also creates *your* window for observation, reflection, or simply catching your breath.

Yes, three hours might sound like a lot at first—but that doesn't mean your child will be working with materials the entire time. The cycle includes set-up, movement, breaks, and moments of stillness. Your job isn't to fill the time with activities—it's to *hold the space* so your child can move through it with autonomy.

In the early days, the bigger challenge may be your own restlessness. It's tempting to interrupt, offer help, or pivot to other tasks. But your calm, consistent presence is part of the environment. Think of this as a discipline you build for yourself, too.

You won't get everything done every day. That's okay. Montessori homeschooling isn't about achieving perfect balance—it's about designing a rhythm that honors your child's learning *and* your family's life. With intention, consistency, and a bit of flexibility, you'll find your footing.

Let's Talk Money!

Let's talk money—because yes, Montessori materials can be expensive, and that reality can feel overwhelming when you're just starting out. There's a common misconception that Montessori homeschooling has to mean investing in an entire classroom's worth of specialized materials. But that's not the case—and more importantly, that's not what makes Montessori *work*.

Montessori is first and foremost about intentionality. The value comes not from having a perfectly stocked shelf, but from choosing high-quality, purposeful materials that meet your child where they are developmentally. You don't need to buy it all at once—or ever. You start with what matters most, based on your child's needs, and build slowly from there.

Here's the truth: thoughtful, strategic choices are always better than hasty overhauls. Buy fewer things, but choose them well. The golden beads and sandpaper letters, for example, are often worth the investment because they support foundational concepts in math and language. But many other items—trays, baskets, pouring tools—can be sourced secondhand, borrowed, or DIYed without compromising the experience.

Tip: What Are Golden Beads and Sandpaper Letters?

Golden beads are foundational Montessori Math materials used to concretely introduce the decimal system and place value (units, tens, hundreds, thousands). They serve as the entry point for nearly all Montessori Math concepts. Children use them to physically build and manipulate large quantities, helping them internalize abstract concepts through hands-on experience. This work prepares the mind for more advanced, abstract learning in later materials.

Sandpaper letters are tactile, foundational language materials that help children associate letter sounds with symbols. As children trace each letter with their fingers while voicing the corresponding sounds, they engage multiple senses—supporting strong phonetic awareness and laying the groundwork for reading and writing.

What matters most is *how* you use the materials, not *how many* you have. And sometimes, investing in your own learning—through books, workshops, or guidance—is more impactful than investing in stuff. You are your child's greatest resource. Your clarity, confidence, and consistency will shape their learning far more than any set of wooden knobs.

If you do choose to purchase materials, do it with intention. Use a scope and sequence to guide your decisions. Borrow or trade with other homeschoolers. Buy secondhand when possible. And if you need a little more structure to get started—yes, even an open-and-go curriculum—use it as a bridge, not a destination. It's okay to meet yourself where you are, as long as you stay aware of where you're headed.

Montessori isn't all-or-nothing. It's about alignment, not perfection. Keep your focus on preparing yourself, observing your child, and curating an environment that evolves with them. That's where the real investment lies—and the return is lifelong.

What Comes Next

Fear and self-doubt are natural parts of this journey. But they don't have to define it. Every Montessori parent, even the most experienced ones, started exactly where you are—wondering if they were capable, questioning if they have what it takes to "do it right." The difference between uncertainty and confidence isn't knowing all the answers—it's trusting yourself to learn, adapt, and grow.

Confidence is not the absence of fear—it's the decision to move forward with intention *despite* it.

As you move deeper into this journey, remember: The real work of Montessori homeschooling isn't about knowing everything—it's about becoming someone who is willing to learn.

You are enough. And you're not alone.

Let's keep going.

Thoughts from the Frontlines

Reflections on moving through fear, quieting self-doubt, and finding the confidence to homeschool with clarity and commitment.

Destiny: Single mother, determined guide

"My biggest fear wasn't whether I *could* homeschool—it was whether I could do it at the level I envisioned. I wanted to offer my son something that rivaled the best private schools, and that takes resources. What helped me move forward was investing in support. Once I had a guide and could see what was possible, I stopped second-guessing myself and started building something sustainable."

Wennie: Nurse and mom of two, carrying the weight of expectations

"As a working mom in a small apartment with two young kids, I kept asking myself—can I really do this? There were so many voices, internal and external, questioning the decision. But I realized if I didn't commit fully and grow my confidence, I'd be swayed too easily.

(continued)

(continued)

Choosing to invest in support was the turning point. I finally stopped trying to do it all alone."

Julianne: Irish minimalist, confronting guilt

"My biggest fear was that I might fail my daughter. Homeschooling is rare here, and I worried I was making the wrong choice. I kept asking, 'What if I'm holding her back?' But once I found our local co-op and connected with others, the doubt quieted. I started to feel capable— not just as her parent, but as her guide."

Wilka: Latina Filipina mom, shifting identity

"I worried I wasn't qualified. I had no formal training, and I kept thinking, what if I'm not enough? But as I learned more, I started to see that Montessori isn't about being the expert—it's about learning *with* your child. That shift helped me release the pressure and show up more fully."

Mae-Lin: Veteran mom, healing from perfectionism

"I used to think I had to be the perfect guide before I could begin. If I didn't understand a lesson perfectly, I couldn't move forward. It took therapy, nervous system work, and a lot of reflection to realize I was still operating from fear. The real breakthrough came when I allowed myself to *start messy*. I wasn't behind. I was exactly where I needed to be."

Tiffany: Bilingual mom of three, learning as she leads

"There were so many doubts at the beginning—about the method, about time, about whether I could really lead my kids through all of this. I still have questions, but I've learned that consistency matters more than perfection. I don't have to know everything to be a good guide. I just have to keep showing up."

To learn more about the families featured throughout this book, you'll find their bios in the appendix.

Note

1. Brené Brown, *The Gifts of Imperfection* (Center City, MN: Hazelden, 2010), 25.

4

Finding Your Why

Defining the Heart of Your Montessori Homeschool

When you decide to homeschool—especially using the Montessori method—it's more than an educational choice. It's a personal, values-based commitment. You're not just choosing *how* your child will learn—you're choosing *why*. That clarity matters.

Understanding your motivation isn't a fluffy, philosophical exercise—it's your foundation. On the hard days (and there will be hard days), your "why" becomes your anchor. On the good days, it becomes your fuel.

This chapter helps you name your purpose, align your approach, and reconnect with what matters most—so your Montessori homeschool isn't just something you do. It's something you *live*.

Why Clarity Comes First

Montessori is not plug-and-play. It's not a boxed curriculum or a rigid checklist. It's a living, breathing way of seeing the child—and that means it's deeply personal.

If you don't know *why* you're doing this, it's easy to:

- Burn out when things get messy
- Second-guess yourself when people question your choices
- Drift toward convenience over intention
- Get lost in trends instead of staying grounded in philosophy

But when your "why" is strong, you'll:

- Make better decisions about what really matters
- Stay rooted during uncertainty
- Choose alignment over perfection

Think of your why as your internal compass. This chapter helps you find yours.

Grounding Your Why in What's Best for the Child

It's natural to bring your own history into this journey—many of us were drawn to homeschooling because of our own educational wounds. Maybe you were bullied in school. Maybe you felt unseen, underestimated, or pressured to conform. Maybe you're trying to do what your own parents didn't—or trying to prove something to yourself or someone else.

Those experiences matter. They shaped you. But your child is not an extension of you.

They are not here to fulfill your unfulfilled dreams, to live out your values without question, or to serve as proof that you're doing it "right." Your child is a whole person, undergoing a process of self-construction—just like you are.

Your role is not to mold them, but to support the unfolding of who they already are.

Montessori education is grounded in constructivism—the idea that children build knowledge through experiences, relationships, and active engagement with their environment. They aren't vessels to be filled with your preferences—they are constructors of their own minds.

"Your 'why' must be rooted not in your fears, ego, or nostalgia—but in your child's needs. In their right to grow at their own pace, to make their own discoveries, and to become themselves."

That's what Montessori offers. And that's why you're here.

Reflective Prompts to Clarify Your Why

Take your time with these. Sit with them. Journal through them. Talk them over with a partner or friend. This isn't about getting the "right" answer— it's about getting to the *true* one.

1. *What drew you to homeschooling in the first place?* Was it a desire for more freedom? A mismatch with traditional school? A longing for deeper connection?
2. *What about Montessori excites or inspires you?* Is it the emphasis on independence? The beauty of self-directed learning? The peaceful, purposeful rhythm?
3. *What values do you want to see reflected in your child's education?* Think beyond academics. What kind of person do you want to raise? What virtues matter most to your family?
4. *What qualities do you want to cultivate in yourself as a homeschooling parent?* Patience? Curiosity? Confidence? Resilience? It's not just about the child—it's about who you're becoming too.
5. *What fears or challenges are on your mind?* Be honest. Are you afraid of falling behind? Of being judged? Of losing your identity? Bringing fears into the light helps you respond to them with grace instead of letting them steer the ship.
6. *Is this truly the right path for your child?* Consider their temperament, learning style, social needs, and family dynamics. Are you choosing this for *them*—or for you?

PRO TIP If you're feeling stuck, ask yourself, "If I could guarantee one thing for my child by the end of this journey, what would it be?"

Practical Exercises for Defining Your Why

These exercises help you move from vague ideas to concrete clarity. Try one at a time or choose the one that resonates most right now.

Create Your Homeschool Mission Statement

Use your reflections to write a two-to three-sentence statement that describes:

- What kind of learning environment do you want to create?
- What values will guide your choices?
- What kind of growth do you hope to support in your child?

Example: Our Montessori homeschool is a space where our child can grow in confidence, curiosity, and independence. We are committed to fostering a love of learning, respecting our child's natural rhythm, and building a home culture rooted in purpose and peace.

Write yours somewhere visible. Let it become your compass.

Choose Three Core Values for Your Homeschool

Circle the words that feel most essential to your family's approach. Then choose three that rise to the top.

Examples:

- Independence
- Creativity
- Responsibility
- Respect
- Wonder
- Curiosity
- Simplicity
- Order
- Connection

Once you've chosen your top three, write a simple sentence for each one that explains why it matters to you.

Example: Respect: Because I want my child to know their voice matters—and so does mine.

Visualize Your Ideal Day

Close your eyes. Picture your child in your homeschool space. What are they doing? How do they move through the environment? How do you feel watching them?

Now write down a short narrative or draw a sketch of what that ideal day looks like. Don't aim for fantasy—aim for *alignment*. Let that vision guide how you structure your space, your rhythm, and your expectations.

Define Short- and Long-Term Intentions

You don't need a five-year plan—but having some clarity around your short- and long-term hopes can help you prioritize.

Short-term goals (next one to three months):

- Build a consistent work cycle
- Establish a peaceful morning rhythm
- Strengthen independence through practical life

Tip: What Is Practical Life in Montessori?

Practical life is the heart of early Montessori education. It includes everyday activities that build independence, coordination, concentration, and a sense of responsibility—like pouring, sweeping, buttoning, washing, folding, and caring for the environment and self.

When practicing Montessori at home, it's easy to confuse these with chores. But practical life isn't about getting things done—it's about creating *purposeful, skill-building experiences* that lay the foundation for academic learning. Through repetition, children develop order, focus, fine motor control, and confidence in their ability to contribute meaningfully.

Start simple. Choose real tools, child-sized materials, and tasks your child already sees you doing or needs more practice with. This turns everyday actions into intentional work—and helps your child build true capability, not just "helpfulness on the go." Over time, you'll find yourself stepping back naturally, watching them lead with confidence.

Long-term goals (1+ years):

- Nurture self-motivation and focus
- Create a deeply connected family learning culture
- Prepare the child for lifelong curiosity and contribution

Keep these written down. Revisit them monthly. Let them evolve.

Why Montessori May Align with Your Why

Still wondering how Montessori fits your goals? Let's name some of the qualities that make it such a powerful approach for home educators:

- **Freedom within limits:** Children make real choices within a structured environment. This builds self-trust and discipline.
- **Respect for the whole child:** Montessori isn't just about academics—it's about character, emotion, and purpose.
- **Hands-on, self-paced learning:** Children learn by doing. At their own rhythm. With space to repeat, explore, and master.
- **Prepared environment:** The adult designs the space to meet the child's needs—not the other way around.
- **Practical life integration:** Real skills, real responsibilities, real participation in daily life.

Does that sound like the kind of learning you want for your child? Then you're in the right place.

Your Montessori Why Statement

Use this prompt to capture your motivation in a way that can grow with you:

I'm choosing Montessori homeschooling because I believe in
_____. My goal is to nurture a space where my child can
_____, while staying grounded in _____and
_____. I am committed to _____.

Example: I'm choosing Montessori homeschooling because I believe in raising self-directed, joyful learners. My goal is to nurture a space where my child can explore freely and grow at their own pace, while staying grounded in simplicity and respect. I am committed to guiding with presence, not pressure.

What Comes Next

It's easy to get swept up in shelf setup, curriculum planning, or Instagram-worthy routines. But those are branches. Your *why* is the root.

Return to it when things feel shaky. Revisit it when you need clarity. Rewrite it as your child grows.

Because Montessori isn't just a method—it's a mindset. And when your mindset is anchored in purpose, everything else grows stronger

Thoughts from the Frontlines

Reflections on discovering a deeper purpose and how defining their "why" helped real parents find clarity by focusing on what mattered most for their child's whole development.

Maria Isabel: Multilingual mom in Sweden

"My biggest goal is to give my son an unhurried and happy childhood. Montessori aligned with that intention. It felt like the only approach that truly respected the child—not just in theory, but in daily practice. That's what made it feel right."

Fatema: Former engineer, now full-time mom in Saudi Arabia

"My 'why' was about giving my child more than just academics. I wanted to enlighten him in all aspects of life. Montessori felt like the only method that respected the child deeply enough to do that."

(continued)

(continued)

Viviana: Doctor of nursing practice turned full-time mom and entrepreneur

"My husband and I looked at how we were raised—and what was missing. We didn't want our daughters to struggle through college the way we did, learning how to self-educate too late. We wanted to raise children who knew how to think, not just follow."

Tiffany: Colombian American mom, homeschooling in Spanish and English

"My goal is a peaceful, respectful, and personalized environment where my girls can shine. I want them to love learning—not just perform. Montessori gives us the structure to build that kind of space."

Sarah: Homeschooling four on a hobby farm

"At first, I was worried about academics. I started with a traditional curriculum and used Montessori materials like manipulatives. But I saw the joy drain from my son. I realized I didn't want to reproduce school at home. I wanted the joy, beauty, and developmentally aligned pace that Montessori offers."

Wilka: Puerto Rican–Filipino working mom

"My why is simple: I want to nurture my daughter as a *whole* person—academically, emotionally, socially. Montessori isn't just about what she learns; it's about *who she becomes* while learning."

To learn more about the families featured throughout this book, you'll find their bios in the appendix.

5

In It Together

How to Build a Montessori-Supportive Household

This chapter isn't about relationship advice—I'm not a marriage counselor. But I am a Montessorian. And over the years, I've seen one truth hold steady: the most successful homeschool families aren't necessarily the ones with the most resources or the most experience. They're the ones with the strongest alignment at home. That alignment doesn't mean everyone is an expert in Montessori. It means the adults in the child's life share a vision, communicate with respect, and create space for each other's voices.

Whether you have a fully supportive partner, a curious but cautious spouse, or extended family who will play a role in your child's education, this work matters. You don't need everyone on board all at once. But you do need to make room for honest conversations—and walk forward with clarity, not confusion.

When the Adults Aren't Aligned Yet

It's incredibly common for one parent or caregiver to dive into Montessori first while the other is still unsure. Maybe you've done all the reading and you're ready to go—but your partner hasn't had the same exposure. That doesn't make them resistant. It just means they're at a different point on the journey.

This chapter is here to help you bridge that gap—not through pressure, but through partnership. These conversations aren't about getting permission. They're about building understanding.

Start with Values, Not Logistics

It's tempting to jump straight to lesson plans and outcomes. But lasting alignment is built on shared values:

- What kind of adult do we want our child to become?
- What qualities matter most in our parenting?
- What kind of home culture do we want to cultivate?

When you start here, you're planting the seeds for deeper connection. Montessori can then be introduced as a path that supports those values—not a rigid system or a personal project.

Begin with an open heart and curiosity. You're not there to "convince" your partner of anything; you're there to understand their perspective and create space for them to explore. Seek first to understand rather than to be understood.

Start with thoughtful, values-based questions:

- **"What values do we both want to instill in our child?"**

   Starting with values builds common ground. Tie Montessori principles—independence, empathy, responsibility—back to the long-term character you both want to nurture.
- **"What hesitations or concerns do you have around home-schooling or Montessori?"**

   Give them space to be honest. Most resistance is rooted in uncertainty or lack of exposure, not rejection. Research shows people are more open to change when their fears are respected rather than dismissed.

■ **"What kind of support do you need from me to feel comfortable with this approach?"**

Clarify expectations. This conversation isn't about assigning tasks—it's about making sure no one feels like they're carrying the weight alone.

These questions can lead to deeper dialogue:

■ "What does success look like to you for our child?"
■ "Are there values from your own childhood you hope to pass on?"
■ "How do you see our roles evolving as our child grows?"

These aren't just icebreakers. They're a foundation. The more you understand each other's hopes and fears, the more equipped you'll be to move forward in sync.

Embrace Curiosity and Compassion in Communication

In any conversation about a significant choice, the goal isn't to persuade—it's to connect. As relationship researcher John Gottman reminds us, lasting connection is built on curiosity and compassion.

If your partner raises a concern, look beneath the surface. Ask, "What about that feels important to you?" Instead of rushing to reassure, try to understand what's underneath.

Example: "I know homeschooling is a big shift, and I'm sure it brings up a lot of thoughts. I'd love to hear your perspective so we can work through this together."

When you lead with empathy and respect, your partner is more likely to respond with openness—and to feel like their role in this decision truly matters.

Navigate Common Concerns with Empathy

As you approach this discussion, remember that many of the concerns your partner may raise are ones you likely shared early on. It's natural for big decisions to come with questions, doubts, and fears, and these can be meaningful opportunities for connection when met with empathy. This section walks through a few concerns that often come up in these conversations, and shows how to approach them with empathy:

- Socialization
  - *Concern:* "Will our child miss out on social experiences?"
  - *Reframe:* Montessori homeschooling offers rich, intentional opportunities for connection—often across ages and contexts, not limited to peer groups. Socialization isn't tied to a classroom setting.
  - *What to Say:* "That was one of my concerns too. But I've found that co-ops, sports, and community classes can create deeper relationships without interfering with our child's quality of education—and we get to choose what aligns with our values."
- Finances
  - *Concern:* "Isn't Montessori really expensive?"
  - *Reframe:* It can be—but it doesn't have to be. Many materials can be made, borrowed, or substituted. Montessori is more about how we guide, not what we buy.
  - *What to Say:* "I've been exploring ways we can keep costs low. We can start with what we have, print out many of the activities, and purchase furniture, trays, and baskets second-hand. If we invest in guidance, we can save quite a bit of money in the long run in my learning to prioritize essentials and build slowly, without pressure."
- Structure and Progress
  - *Concern:* "How will we know our child is keeping up?"
  - *Reframe:* Montessori has structure—it's just developmentally aligned rather than standardized. Progress is measured by mastery, not pacing through a checklist.
  - *What to Say:* "Let's give it a trial period and revisit how it's going in six months. We can observe progress together and make adjustments if needed."

As you approach these discussions, stay tuned to your partner's reactions. If they seem receptive, build on the conversation with examples and further reassurance. If they appear overwhelmed, remember that there's no rush; consider pausing to give them time to process before revisiting the conversation.

Defining Support and Clarifying Roles

Support doesn't mean splitting tasks evenly or turning your partner into a co-teacher. It means identifying ways they can engage meaningfully—without added pressure or overwhelm.

Support might look like:

- Respecting the flow of the work cycle
- Helping with Practical Life routines like cooking or gardening
- Offering encouragement when your child explores something new
- Taking on certain household responsibilities to protect learning time

Rather than prescribing involvement, frame it as an invitation. Try saying, "Support doesn't mean you need to know everything about Montessori. It could simply mean encouraging our child when they're working on something new or helping protect that quiet time for them to concentrate."

You might ask if they'd like to read a short article, join a field trip, or take the lead on a project over the weekend. Keep it flexible. The goal isn't perfection—it's participation. Clarifying roles in this way relieves pressure and builds a rhythm of support that everyone can sustain.

Knowing When to Pause and Revisit the Conversation

Big decisions stir up big feelings. And conversations about homeschooling—especially something as different as Montessori—can surface long-held beliefs, personal fears, or even unresolved experiences from our own childhoods. If your partner is unsure or resistant, know this: it's okay to slow down.

Alignment doesn't happen in one conversation. It's built over time through mutual trust, curiosity, and space to reflect. If you sense the discussion becoming tense or your partner pulling back—short answers, crossed arms, checked-out body language—take a breath. A gentle pause can make all the difference.

You might say, "I can see this feels like a lot to take in. Let's take a break and circle back to it in a few days." That one sentence signals respect, eases pressure, and shows that you're committed to collaboration, not control.

When you're ready to revisit the conversation, set a clear time: "How about we check in this weekend? I'd love to hear what's been on your mind." These micro-boundaries allow the conversation to breathe—and remind both of you that it's a shared journey, not a solo decision.

Grace and Courtesy in Real Life

Grace and courtesy aren't just Montessori lessons for children—they're everyday tools for adults, too. The emotional environment you and your partner create together will shape your child's experience as much as the materials on the shelf.

If tension is running high, it's okay to acknowledge it. But remember: grace means showing kindness to yourself in the process. Courtesy means showing the same to others. You're not going to have every conversation go perfectly. That's not the goal. The goal is to stay connected even in disagreement—to model respect, patience, and emotional maturity, just as you hope your child will someday.

Start by leading with presence, not persuasion. "I want to understand how you're feeling about all this" goes much further than "Here's why I'm right." Respect, in Montessori, is not something to be earned. It's something we offer—freely, consistently, and without conditions. That mindset is what builds emotional safety and trust at home.

Creating an Environment of Unity

Children are remarkably attuned to the emotional landscape of the home. When the adults around them move in sync—grounded, respectful, and calm—it gives them a sense of safety that no shelf or lesson can replicate. But when there's ongoing disagreement or stress, children pick up on that, too—and it can disrupt their ability to learn, focus, and feel secure.

You don't need to agree on every detail to build unity. You just need to align on your shared vision and be intentional in how you present that vision to others. If extended family questions your choices, you don't owe them an explanation. You owe your child a consistent, secure environment.

When boundary-setting becomes necessary, do it with grace. "We've made this decision together, and we're committed to it" is often enough. If needed, redirect conversations that become critical or unproductive. Your confidence doesn't have to be loud—it just has to be steady.

Over time, these boundaries become second nature. The more you trust your path, the less you feel the need to defend it. And in that space, your child thrives—because they're surrounded by adults who are calm, clear, and connected.

Holding Boundaries with Extended Family

Sometimes, the hard conversations don't stop at home. Once you've made the decision to homeschool, family and friends may have strong opinions—and they may not always be supportive. That's okay. Your job isn't to convince them. It's to protect your peace and maintain alignment with your partner.

When these conversations arise, treat them as boundary-setting moments—not debates. You might say:

- "We've chosen a path that really aligns with our values."
- "Thanks for sharing your perspective—we've put a lot of thought into this."
- Or, simply: "I've got this."

When necessary, redirect with grace: "I don't think this conversation is helpful right now. Let's change the subject."

Over time, these boundaries become more natural. You'll become less reactive and more rooted in the confidence that you *know* your child and what they need. And that confidence will make space for deeper trust in yourself—and in your partner.

What Comes Next

You don't need perfect conversations to move forward. You need consistent, respectful ones. You need time. And you need the willingness to keep coming back to the table—even if the conversations are imperfect, messy, or unresolved at first.

I continue this conversation in Chapter 21, where you'll explore how to adapt Montessori to your family's reality without losing the depth or integrity of the method.

Remember, Montessori is a lifelong journey—not just for your child, but for you and your family. Every thoughtful pause, every moment of listening, every time you choose understanding over urgency—that's a lesson in grace. And it's one your whole family will benefit from.

This work isn't about having all the answers. It's about walking forward with clarity, even when the path is still unfolding. You're learning to trust yourself so that your child can trust the world around them. And that is powerful.

Thoughts from the Frontlines

Montessori thrives when the whole household is aligned—not perfect, but purposeful. Hear how real families create supportive rhythms, share the mental load, and build systems that make Montessori sustainable for everyone involved.

Viviana: Romanian-Albanian mom of three, small business owner

"I observe my children's behaviors, emotions, and how it's all affecting our day and our life. Then I take those observations and discuss them with my husband. Usually it's on our date night or Sundays—what's working, what isn't, and what needs to shift. That's how we stay aligned as a family."

Tiffany: Bilingual homeschooler raising three daughters

"My husband wasn't always in the loop, and I felt like I had to carry everything. That changed when we started using a shared calendar. Now he knows what's going on and can take on more. It's been huge—for my mental load, our teamwork, and our consistency."

Destiny: Single mom building a Montessori life with intention

"I have a tight-knit circle of friends and family who step in when I need time to prep or rest. Whether it's cutting materials or watching my son during planning time, that community support makes all of this possible. Montessori might happen in my home—but I don't do it alone."

Mae-Lin: Military veteran and homeschooling mom

"We forget how many roles we're juggling: parent, guide, peer, house manager. If I don't take care of myself—therapy, nervous system regulation, boundaries—everything else breaks down. My ability to support my daughter depends on how well I support myself."

Wennie: Nurse and Montessori homeschooler of two

"I work part-time and homeschool two young kids. My husband and I had to set clear rhythms and boundaries. That included deciding what we could say no to, and how we'd organize our time. It's not perfect, but it's ours—and it works because we're on the same page."

To learn more about the families featured throughout this book, you'll find their bios in the appendix.

SECTION 2

How Montessori Works

Understanding the Philosophy So You Can Apply It with Confidence

You've laid the groundwork. You've clarified your *why*. Now it's time to build your understanding of *how* Montessori actually works—so you can guide your child with confidence and clarity.

This section is your bridge between inspiration and implementation. If you've ever asked:

- How is Montessori really different from traditional school?
- What role do I play as the adult?
- How do I balance freedom with structure?
- How do I know what my child is ready for?

then you're exactly where you need to be.

This section begins by examining how Montessori differs from conventional education—not just in terms of structure or method, but in its entire purpose. Montessori isn't about managing behavior or delivering content. It's about supporting the full development of the human being—mind, body, and spirit.

From there, I break down the *three pillars of Montessori:* the child, the environment, and the prepared adult. You'll learn what each of these elements really means, how they interact, and how to support them at home—*without* replicating a classroom.

You'll also explore one of the most misunderstood ideas in Montessori: *freedom within limits.* I walk through how to offer real choice without chaos, how to hold boundaries with grace, and how this balance is what actually builds independence—not undermines it.

Finally, you'll dive into *Montessori's Four Planes of Development*—a framework that helps you understand *why* children behave the way they do, *what* they need at each stage, and *how* to meet those needs with confidence. You'll begin to see your child not as someone to manage, but as someone *becoming*—and that shift changes everything.

By the end of this section, you won't just understand Montessori as a theory. You'll see it as a living, responsive system that helps you meet your child where they are—and grow alongside them, with purpose.

This is the part where things start to click.

Let's get into it.

6

Montessori vs. Traditional Education

Why Montessori Isn't Just Another Teaching Method

When most people think about education, a familiar picture comes to mind: rows of desks, a teacher at the front of the room, students receiving information. The focus tends to be on what to teach, how to teach it, and when students should learn it. That's the model many of us grew up with—a system built on efficiency, order, and outcomes.

Montessori offers something entirely different.

It's not just a different method—it's a different mindset. A different definition of education.

Instead of seeing children as empty vessels to be filled, Montessori sees them as active participants in their own development. Instead of structuring learning around externally imposed benchmarks, Montessori organizes education around natural human development. It's not just about transferring information—it's about unfolding potential.

If you've felt drawn to Montessori but struggled to understand why it feels so different from what you're used to, this chapter helps make that difference clear. Let's explore how Montessori and traditional education differ—not just in style, but in substance.

Traditional Education: Delivering Knowledge

Traditional education is designed like a factory. It begins with a standardized curriculum—decided by someone far removed from your child—and delivers it to students based on age, not readiness. The teacher is positioned at the front of the classroom, responsible for managing behavior, delivering content, and ensuring all students move through the material at the same pace.

Imagine a conveyor belt. Each child is a product moving down the line. If a student falls behind, the belt keeps moving. If they move ahead, they're often told to wait. It's a system that prioritizes efficiency over individuality.

Success is measured by compliance, grades, and test scores. Curiosity is often sacrificed for control. And while this structure may feel predictable and familiar, it rarely supports the unique developmental needs of each child.

As Mario Montessori, the son of Dr. Montessori, described, traditional pedagogy is driven by three questions:

- What should be taught?
- How should it be taught?
- Who should be taught what?

Montessori turns those questions inside out.

Montessori: Supporting Human Development

Montessori education doesn't start with the curriculum—it starts with the child.

Dr. Maria Montessori's most famous insight was simple but revolutionary: "I discovered the child." Rather than asking what to teach and when, Montessori asks: What does the child need in order to grow? How can we support—not direct—their natural development?

Maria Montessori explained that education cannot be separated from the broader process of human development. She wrote, "To understand the child's tendencies with the purpose of educating him, we must see man in correlation with his environment and how his adaptation to it is created."[1]

Montessori is rooted in the belief that education should be an aid to life. That means it must support the whole child: their body, their mind, their heart, and their spirit. It's not about checking boxes or racing through content. It's about becoming—becoming independent, curious, responsible, and capable.

That's why the adult is called a guide in Montessori, not a teacher. The guide prepares the environment and carefully observes the child, offering just the right lessons at just the right time—not to impose learning, but to spark it.

What Makes Montessori So Different?

This section walks through a few side-by-side comparisons to illustrate how Montessori departs from the traditional school model.

The Role of the Adult

- **Traditional Education:** The teacher delivers content, controls the pace, and evaluates performance. Picture a teacher standing at the whiteboard, speaking while a class of 25 children sits in rows of desks, silently taking notes. The room buzzes with the sound of pencils scratching and the occasional cough. The teacher moves quickly, managing time and behavior to stay "on track." The children are listeners, not participants.

- **Montessori:** The guide prepares the environment, observes the child, and offers support when needed. Their job is to remove obstacles, not deliver content. A Montessori guide might sit quietly nearby while a child pours water from one pitcher to another—observing readiness, not correcting technique. The room is hushed but alive with movement. Children choose their work, and the adult's presence is grounded, calm, and attentive.

The Learning Process

- **Traditional Education:** Learning is passive. Children receive information and are expected to memorize and recall it. Picture students filling in worksheets, copying notes from the board, or completing spelling drills. The same task, done by everyone, at the same time.

- **Montessori:** Learning is active. Children learn by doing—by exploring, manipulating, and discovering through hands-on materials. A child using golden beads to build numbers isn't just memorizing math—they're internalizing it through movement and repetition. You'll see a child carefully count out 10 golden beads, grouping them into units, tens, hundreds—then trading them out for colored number cards. They are building concepts from the ground up, one bead at a time.

Curriculum and Pace

- **Traditional Education:** Everyone learns the same thing at the same time, regardless of interest or readiness. A six-year-old will be assessed on addition by the end of their first-grade year, even if they're still mastering number sense—or already doing multiplication. The goal is that everyone performs to a predetermined standard, not necessarily that they learn. The teacher is focused on delivering lessons that are engaging enough to gain compliance, following a checklist that ensures each child is covering the same material at the same time.
- **Montessori:** Education is individualized, and the goal is for children to learn how to learn. Children move through carefully sequenced lessons at their own pace, following developmental readiness and personal curiosity. A child might spend weeks immersed in the bead chains, not because they're "behind," but because they're building a strong foundation. One child might explore number concepts through hands-on decimal work while another is still solidifying place value. Both are learning exactly what they need when they're ready. The guide is focused on helping children think critically, make decisions, and self-organize—not just complete tasks.

Montessori understands learning not as standards to be met, but as markers or milestones aligned to the student's plane of development.

The Environment

- **Traditional Education:** Classrooms are designed for efficiency and control—rows of desks, bright visuals, a clock on the wall, and a bell to signal transitions. The classroom layout is adult-centered: bulletin boards remind students of rules and key facts; desks are arranged for ease of supervision, not collaboration. Primary colors dominate the room to energize students and maintain attention, often overwhelming rather than calming.

- **Montessori:** The environment is calm, ordered, and intentional. The space is designed for the child—with soft, neutral colors, natural light, and gentle textures that soothe rather than stimulate.[2] Materials are carefully arranged on low shelves, each with a distinct purpose. There is space to move, space to work, space to reflect. The result is an environment that invites deep focus and respectful independence.

Motivation and Assessment

- **Traditional Education:** Motivation is external—grades, stickers, praise, rewards, and consequences. Assessment is standardized, often high-stakes. Students are encouraged to participate in fundraisers and rewarded with pizza parties or limo rides for selling the most candy. Recess supervisors hand out tickets to reinforce compliance; primary teachers offer stars and stamps for good behavior. Testing measures comparison more than growth—and reinforces a culture of performance over mastery.

- **Montessori:** Motivation is internal. Children are driven by mastery, curiosity, and meaningful work. Assessment is ongoing and observational. A guide notices patterns in behavior, tracks progress, and adapts support accordingly. When a child struggles with care of environment, they receive a grace and courtesy lesson—not a scolding. When they succeed, the reward is in the experience itself: the satisfaction of pouring water without spilling, of finishing a long work cycle, of taking responsibility for their space. Natural consequences and respect-based redirection guide behavior—not punishments or rewards.

Montessori-Inspired vs. Montessori-Aligned vs. Authentic Montessori vs. High-Integrity Montessori

If you've browsed Pinterest or social media, you've probably seen the terms Montessori-inspired or Montessori-aligned. But what do they mean?

- **Montessori-inspired** usually refers to activities that look Montessori—wooden toys, natural colors, maybe some trays or baskets—but don't necessarily follow the deeper philosophy. It's often more about the aesthetic than the function.
- **Montessori-aligned** means an effort is being made to respect the core principles, even if not all components are present. This might look like following the child's interest and offering hands-on materials, even if they aren't traditional Montessori ones.
- **Authentic Montessori** follows the full approach: the philosophy, the sequence, the role of the adult, the materials, and the environment—all working together in harmony.
- **High-integrity Montessori** is a useful term for homeschoolers. It acknowledges that while a home might not replicate a classroom in full, the family is committed to preserving the method's core values. This means making intentional choices, preparing the adult as much as the space, and aligning decisions with Montessori's purpose, not just its appearance.

You don't have to do everything perfectly from the start. But the more you understand the why behind the method, the more aligned your approach will become—and the more you'll see the transformation unfold.

Why This Matters for You

As a homeschooling parent, this comparison matters. It's not just about choosing a different curriculum—it's about choosing a different paradigm. Montessori asks you to:

- Trust in your child's natural development.
- Observe before acting.
- Offer meaningful, developmentally appropriate work.
- Respect your child's pace, personality, and process.

This might feel unfamiliar at first—especially if you grew up in a traditional school system. You may worry that your child will fall behind or that you're "not doing enough." But Montessori invites you to see growth through a different lens: curiosity, concentration, compassion, and confidence.

What Comes Next

Montessori is not about rejecting structure. It's about creating structure that actually serves the child. It replaces rigid systems with intentional environments. It honors curiosity. It builds lifelong learners.

You don't need to replicate a classroom. You need to prepare a space where learning can unfold naturally.

The next chapter breaks down exactly how Montessori works—through its three foundational pillars: the child, the guide, and the environment. These pillars are what make the method so powerful, and so possible, to implement at home.

Let's take a closer look.

Thoughts from the Frontlines

Montessori isn't just swapping one set of instructions for another—it's a different way to think about learning. Hear how real families let go of traditional schooling mindsets and embraced a more intentional, child-centered approach.

Sarah: Homeschooling mother of four on a small hobby farm
"When I was using a traditional curriculum, it sucked the joy out of learning for both of us. My son was doing the work, but the light was gone. Once I stepped fully into Montessori, it felt like we were finally moving in the direction that honored who he actually was."

Wilka: Multicultural mom of one, working part-time
"My first year of Montessori homeschooling, I didn't realize how much I was approaching it like school—with checklists and control. I was treating it like a method instead of a mindset. Once I shifted, it was like something unlocked. Montessori isn't school at home—it's a whole different way of seeing the child."

Viviana: Romanian-Albanian mom of three
"My husband and I both went through traditional schooling. It wasn't until we researched Montessori that we realized how much we'd

(continued)

(continued)

missed—real independence, self-direction, critical thinking. We don't want our daughters to spend their whole lives unlearning what they were taught."

Mae-Lin—Veteran and first-time homeschooler

"What changed everything for me was realizing how much Montessori is built on human development. It's not just about academics or behavior—it's about the whole child. Traditional education felt like delivering information. Montessori feels like an invitation to become."

Julianne: Montessori homeschooling mom in Northern Ireland

"The more we learned about Montessori, the more we saw how aligned it was with our lifestyle and values. It made us question what education was really for. Not just content mastery—but self-mastery, curiosity, autonomy. That's what we want for our daughter."

To learn more about the families featured throughout this book, you'll find their bios in the appendix.

Notes

1. Maria Montessori, *The 1946 London Lectures* (Lynne Lawrence, Amsterdam: Montessori-Pierson Publishing Company, 2012), 101.
2. This emphasis on calm, neutral colors, natural light, and intentional design is not just stylistic—it's supported by developmental psychology and environmental research. A thoughtfully prepared space reduces cognitive overload, nurtures emotional regulation, and invites concentration through clarity not clutter.

7 | The Three Pillars of Montessori

The Child, the Guide, and the Environment

In the early days of my Montessori journey, I remember watching my child struggle to tie her shoes. My instinct was to jump in—to fix it, to smooth it over, to keep things moving. But something told me to pause. I had just read about the importance of letting children experience productive struggle, and so I waited. She fumbled. Tried again. Frowned. And then—slowly, clumsily—she figured it out. Her face lit up. And I realized: *This is the work.*

Montessori is built on moments like these—quiet, everyday moments that honor the child's ability to grow, learn, and overcome with support rather than interference. These moments don't happen by accident. They arise when three essential elements work in harmony: *the child, the guide,* and *the environment.*

These three pillars are the foundation of Montessori. Not just a method. A living, breathing system. When they're aligned, learning becomes something the child owns—something that sparks from within rather than being imposed from outside. This chapter explores what each of these pillars really means and how they work together to create the kind of learning you probably wish *you* had growing up.

Pillar 1: The Child—The Center of Their Own Learning

Think back to a time when your child got completely absorbed in something—pouring water between cups, stacking blocks, arranging figurines just so. That wasn't wasted time. That was concentration. Purposeful work. Self-construction.

Montessori sees the child as a full person—driven by an inner force to grow and learn. Dr. Maria Montessori wrote, "The child is both a hope and a promise for mankind." This isn't poetic idealism—it's a call to observe children as capable, active participants in their own development.

Rather than fill children with knowledge, we follow their natural drive to explore. They lead, we follow—not passively, but with deep awareness of their developmental needs.

Practical ways to support this:

- Observe more than you intervene. What holds their focus? Where do they persist?
- Follow their interests, but guide them toward meaningful work.
- Create a rhythm that honors concentration and limits interruptions.
- Trust that your child has their own internal timeline—and it might not look like anyone else's.

Pillar 2: The Guide—Supporting Without Controlling

We all want to help our children succeed—but Montessori asks us to redefine help. Sometimes helping looks like *not* stepping in. It looks like giving just enough support, then stepping back so the child can do the work of growing.

As Montessori adults, we're not the center of the learning experience. We're not there to perform, direct, or control. We are there to *observe*, to *prepare*, and to *get out of the way* when the child is ready to act.

Dr. Maria Montessori described the adult's role as "an intelligent observer and guide." That means knowing when to speak and when to stay silent, when to demonstrate and when to let the child discover. This requires patience and self-awareness. It's easy to fall into the habit of giving too many instructions or expecting immediate results.

"Stepping back intentionally allows children to develop resilience, confidence, and a sense of ownership over their learning."

Practical ways to guide:

- Model skills slowly and silently. Let your hands do the talking.
- Avoid correcting right away—especially if it interrupts the child's process.
- Ask fewer questions. Make fewer suggestions. Watch more.
- Accept the child's pace—even when it's slower than you think it should be.

Pillar 3: The Environment—The Silent Teacher

Children don't need a playroom full of toys. They need a space that invites them to explore with purpose. In Montessori, the environment is not a backdrop—it's an active part of the learning process.

When the environment is calm, orderly, and intentional, it communicates: *You belong here. You can do this. This space is for you.*

Montessori classrooms (and home environments) are thoughtfully prepared to offer freedom within limits. Everything is accessible. Materials are beautiful and purposeful. There's room to move. There's quiet. There's order. The space itself teaches.

Practical ways to prepare the environment:

- Use low shelves and trays to encourage independence.
- Reduce clutter. Offer fewer materials—but choose them carefully.
- Use calming colors and natural lighting when possible.

Ask:

- **Accessibility:** Can my child reach and use this independently?
- **Order:** Is it obvious where things belong?
- **Purpose:** Does this material support a real developmental need?
- **Preparation:** Does this activity include everything my child needs to work without help?

Why All Three Pillars Matter

Montessori is not child-led chaos. It's not adult-led instruction. And it's not just minimalist design. It's a balance—a living system in which the child, the guide, and the environment work together.

When the guide is prepared, the environment is intentional, and the child is respected, *real* learning happens. Learning that's joyful. Deep. Self-motivated. Lasting. Mario Montessori said it plainly: "The first step in the education of the child is the adaptation of the adult."

This work begins with us.

What Comes Next

You don't need all the materials. You don't need the perfect shelf. You don't need to be a certified teacher. What you *do* need is a solid understanding of these three pillars—and a willingness to keep showing up.

Montessori isn't about control. It's about connection.

Connection between child and guide.
Between guide and environment.
Between the child and their unfolding potential.

These three pillars don't stand alone—they move in harmony. When one shifts, the others respond. It's a fluid dance, not a fixed formula. And it's in this movement that growth happens—for your child, and for you.

The next chapter discusses the role that matters most in a Montessori homeschool: yours. Because the real foundation of this work isn't materials. It's YOU.

Thoughts from the Frontlines

Stories about how real families discovered the power of aligning the child, the guide, and the environment, and how that harmony transforms not just learning, but daily life.

Wilka: Multicultural mom of one, working part-time

"I used to think being a good homeschool parent meant having all the answers. But Montessori taught me that my role isn't to be the expert—it's to observe, to prepare, and to trust. That shift from controlling to guiding changed everything in how I relate to my daughter."

Wennie: Nurse and homeschooling mom of two in a small apartment

"The child, the guide, and the environment—once I understood that triangle, I realized how each part needs to be in harmony. When I prepared myself and the space with intention, my kids naturally stepped into deeper focus and independence."

Mae-Lin: Army veteran and mother of one

"I didn't know how much I was expecting my daughter to perform for me—until I realized I wasn't showing up as the kind of guide she needed. Now I say to myself every day, *I am part of the environment.* If I'm dysregulated, the whole system gets off balance. So I lead by calming myself first."

Tiffany: Colombian-American mom of three

"With three young kids at home, I've learned that preparing the environment isn't about perfection—it's about alignment. When the shelves are intentional and the rhythm is clear, my daughters settle in naturally. The adult sets the tone, the environment holds the structure, and the child gets to thrive."

Destiny: Single mom and cultural educator

"The three pillars made me realize that my presence—not just my planning—was the most powerful part of the homeschool. I had to stop trying to get it all 'right' and start showing up fully as a guide, an anchor, a model. That's what holds the environment steady."

To learn more about the families featured throughout this book, you'll find their bios in the appendix.

8

The Prepared Adult

Why Your Growth Matters More Than Any Curriculum

When parents begin their Montessori homeschooling journey, the first questions are almost always logistical:

What should I teach? When do I introduce this material? Where do I get the right curriculum?

These questions make sense—especially if you're coming from a traditional schooling background, where education is structured around pacing guides and externally designed lesson plans. But Montessori is different. It doesn't begin with a curriculum. It begins with you.

Montessori homeschooling isn't built on scripts or standards—it's built on the internal preparation of the adult. You are the curriculum's most important component. Your mindset, your presence, your ability to observe, respond, and prepare the environment—all of these are what make Montessori education come alive at home.

This chapter isn't about what your child needs to learn. It's about who you need to become.

Because Montessori homeschooling doesn't succeed on materials alone—it succeeds on your commitment to growth, clarity, and becoming the adult your child needs.

The Adult as Leader and Observer

One of the most important shifts in Montessori homeschooling is this: You are not a traditional teacher. You are a prepared observer—a responsive guide.

Dr. Maria Montessori famously said, "Follow the child—but follow them as their leader."

You're not delivering content. You're not the keeper of all knowledge. You're creating the conditions for learning—offering the right experiences at the right time, noticing what calls to your child, and adjusting the environment accordingly.

Observation isn't passive—it's active, intentional, and scientific. You gather information, make thoughtful decisions, and guide gently. If your child resists a lesson, you don't double down—you ask why. If they're struggling with fine motor skills, you don't rush to handwriting worksheets—you offer practical life work that strengthens their hand.

You aren't controlling the process—you're supporting it. And that requires trust. In the child. In the method. And in yourself.

The Adult as Emotional Anchor

Montessori education is holistic. It nurtures not just the intellect, but the whole child—body, heart, and mind, which means your presence matters more than your teaching technique.

You are the emotional anchor in your home. Your child looks to you not just for guidance, but for safety, steadiness, and trust. That doesn't mean you need to be perfect. It means you need to be present.

A prepared adult brings emotional availability to the learning environment. You're calm when they're overwhelmed. You offer compassion when they stumble. You model patience when things don't go as planned. When your child feels safe, they are free to take risks—and learning is a series of small, meaningful risks.

To show up this way, you also need to care for *yourself*. Burnout, resentment, and constant overwhelm are not badges of honor—they're barriers to connection. Montessori homeschooling asks for your presence, not your perfection. The more grounded you are, the more grounded your child will be.

The Adult as Creator of the Prepared Environment

Montessori focuses a lot on the prepared environment. But let's clarify what that actually means at home.

The prepared environment is more than a shelf or a corner of the living room—it's a way of designing your space to support independence, curiosity, and responsibility. It evolves with your child. It reflects their needs—not your aesthetic.

You don't need a room full of expensive materials. What you need is intentionality. Chapter 7 covered the four qualities that define a Montessori-ready space: accessibility, order, purpose, and preparation. These same principles apply here—because creating a prepared environment isn't just about what's on the shelf. It's about how you support your child's independence through thoughtful design and your own steady presence.

Your kitchen becomes a site for practical life. Your backyard becomes a space for movement and exploration. Your bookshelf becomes a tool for literacy, storytelling, and imagination.

When you're homeschooling, a part of your home is dedicated to study. Think of it like the old-fashioned study room—an intentional space that communicates the purpose of learning. This helps the environment itself guide the child in understanding the expectations of the work cycle.

Dr. Maria Montessori reminds us:

> "The first thing [a child's] education demands is the provision of an environment in which he can develop the powers given him by nature. This does not mean just to amuse him and let him do what he likes. But it does mean that we have to adjust our minds to doing a work of collaboration with nature. . . the law which decrees that development comes from environmental experience."[1]

Creating and maintaining the environment is a core part of your role—not just because it facilitates learning, but because it communicates trust: *I believe in your ability to do things for yourself.*

The Adult as Role Model and Mentor

In Montessori, children learn by watching the adults around them. You are their blueprint—not just for behavior, but for habits of mind.

- If you want your child to respect others' time and space, *practice that same respect in your interactions.*
- If you want them to develop focus, model deep concentration in your own work and hobbies.
- If you want them to handle mistakes with grace, *show them how you respond to your own setbacks.*

Montessori calls this indirect preparation. You're not giving a lesson—you're living the example.

Your discipline becomes theirs. Your curiosity becomes theirs. Your self-regulation becomes the foundation for their own. That's the power—and responsibility—of the prepared adult.

The Adult as Co-Learner

One of the most freeing truths about Montessori homeschooling is this: You don't need to know everything. In fact, approaching learning as a co-learner—rather than an authority figure—can be one of your most powerful tools.

When you shift from directing lessons to sharing them, everything changes. Lessons become shared experiences. Questions become opportunities for connection. And your curiosity becomes contagious.

When you say, "I don't know—let's find out together," you're not revealing a weakness. You're modeling intellectual humility. You're showing your child that learning is a lifelong journey—not something that ends in adulthood.

Your willingness to try, to be wrong, to stay curious—these are the habits that cultivate confidence, resilience, and joy. And when your child sees you learning, growing, and even struggling with something new, they internalize an essential truth: *It's safe to learn here.*

You don't need to be an expert. You just need to be engaged. And when you learn together, you build trust—not just in the method, but in each other.

The Adult as a Work in Progress

Let's be clear: There's no such thing as a perfectly prepared adult.

There will be days when you feel distracted, impatient, or discouraged. There will be lessons that flop, routines that unravel, and moments when you wonder if this was the right choice.

That's not a sign of failure. That's a sign you're growing.

Montessori homeschooling is a mirror. It will reflect back your habits, assumptions, and beliefs about control, productivity, and success. That's not always comfortable—but it is transformative.

Your child is learning how to be human by watching *you* be human. Not flawless—*authentic*. When you show up with humility, self-compassion, and a willingness to try again, you model the very mindset that allows deep learning to happen. So give yourself permission to grow. To ask for help. To take breaks. To learn alongside your child.

What Comes Next

The Montessori guide is not defined by their materials, their credentials, or their perfectly organized shelves. They are defined by their posture— observant, respectful, curious, and prepared.

As you finish this first section of the book, I want you to let go of the idea that Montessori homeschooling starts with doing it "right."

It starts with *becoming* the prepared adult your child needs.

You don't have to be perfect. But you do need to be intentional. The more you prepare yourself—the more clarity, self-awareness, and trust you build—the more capable you'll be of creating a home environment where Montessori can truly thrive.

And the truth is: That work has already begun.

Let's keep going.

Thoughts from the Frontlines

Montessori doesn't begin with the child's work—it begins with the adult's. Hear how real families shifted their mindset, regulated their presence, and discovered how preparing themselves changed everything in their homeschool.

(continued)

(continued)

Mae-Lin: Army veteran and mother of one

"I thought the hardest part would be the lessons or the materials. But it was me. My mindset. My triggers. I had to regulate my nervous system before I could lead with calm, before I could hold space. I tell myself daily: 'I'm a work in progress—and so is she'. That's Montessori."

Fatema: Former engineer and homeschooling mom of two in Saudi Arabia

"My biggest fear was me—my discipline, my ability to follow through. But I kept coming back to my 'why' and that kept me grounded. I started putting systems in place not just for my child's learning, but for *my* preparation. That's when it all began to shift."

Viviana: Doctor of nursing practice turned stay-at-home mom of three

"I used to think homeschooling was about getting everything right for my daughter. But I've learned it's also about healing myself. Through observation and reflection, I realized I was passing on pressure, not presence. Now I check in with myself first—because I set the tone."

Wilka: Multicultural mom of one

"In our first year, I was treating Montessori like a checklist. It wasn't until I began working on myself—my mindset, my tone, my trust in the process—that things started to click. I had to stop rushing and start *observing*. The prepared adult is not perfect. She's aware."

Tiffany: Colombian-American mom of three

"The hardest thing was just believing I could *do* this. Not because I didn't care, but because I was juggling so much. What helped most was learning that preparation isn't just about the shelves—it's about preparing *myself* to show up with calm, with clarity, and with flexibility."

To learn more about the families featured throughout this book, you'll find their bios in the appendix.

Note

1. Maria Montessori, *The Absorbent Mind*, trans. Claude A. Claremont (New York: Holt, Rinehart and Winston, 1967), 267.

9

Freedom Within Limits

The Balance of Structure and Flexibility

As a new Montessori homeschooling parent, one of the first things you'll hear is: *follow the child*. But what does that actually mean?

For many parents, it sparks confusion. How do you follow the child without giving up structure? How do you let your child lead without everything falling apart into chaos—or feeling like you're just winging it?

The answer lies in one of Montessori's most essential (and misunderstood) principles: *freedom within limits*.

At first, this phrase sounds like a contradiction. Isn't freedom the opposite of limits? But in Montessori, it's the *combination* of the two that creates the conditions for true independence, deep focus, and peaceful coexistence. Think of it as a dance: the child moves with freedom, but the rhythm is set by a structure that supports—not controls—their growth.

This chapter is your guide to understanding what freedom within limits really means, why it's essential for Montessori at home, and how to apply it to your learning environment and your parenting rhythm.

What Freedom Within Limits Actually Means

In traditional models of education, discipline is often something imposed. Children are told what to do, when to do it, and how to behave—or else. On the flip side, when some parents hear about child-led learning, they interpret it as *anything goes*—letting the child do whatever they want, whenever they want.

Montessori offers a third way. Freedom within limits is not about control, nor is it about chaos. It's about offering *meaningful choice within a well-prepared structure*.

Dr. Maria Montessori explained it this way: "To let the child do as he likes when he has not yet developed the power of control is to betray the idea of freedom."

Freedom in Montessori doesn't mean the absence of boundaries. It means the presence of boundaries that are *clear, consistent*, and *developmentally appropriate*. True freedom comes from the ability to make constructive choices, to follow your interests within a respectful, supportive framework. Without structure, children feel unanchored. Without freedom, they feel stifled. Freedom within limits is how we honor both their autonomy and their need for guidance.

> "Think of freedom within limits as a dance: the child moves with freedom, but the rhythm is set by a structure that supports—not controls—their growth."

The Three Components That Make It Work

To apply freedom within limits in your homeschool, you'll need to think through three elements: the child, the environment, and the adult guide. Sound familiar? These are the same pillars explored in Chapter 7, now put into dynamic relationship.

The Child: Capable, but Still Developing

Children have the drive to grow—but they don't yet have all the skills to regulate themselves. That's where limits come in. Limits don't hinder growth; they support it. They help the child feel secure enough to explore.

Example: A preschooler may freely choose an activity from the shelf, but they learn they must return it to its proper place before choosing another. That limit encourages responsibility and order without punishing curiosity.

The Environment: Designed for Independence

The prepared environment provides natural boundaries. Materials are limited, purposeful, and self-contained. Children are free to choose, but only from options that have been intentionally curated for their developmental needs.

Example: Your child can prepare their own snack from a low shelf, but only after washing their hands and using the appropriate tools. The environment invites freedom, but only after the child engages with its built-in expectations.

The Adult: Calm, Clear, Consistent

As the guide, your role is to observe, set limits that make sense, and follow through with consistency. You're not a micromanager. You're the keeper of structure and tone.

Example: If your child throws a material, you calmly remove it. Not as punishment, but as a logical response: "This work is not for throwing. We can try again tomorrow."

What It Looks Like at Home

Bringing freedom within limits into your Montessori homeschool doesn't require perfection. It just requires clarity and consistency.

In the learning space:

- **Offer limited, intentional choices:** "Would you like to work with the sandpaper letters or the number rods?"

- **Maintain order:** Each activity should have a beginning, middle, and end—and everything the child needs should be included on the tray.
- **Honor concentration:** If your child is focused, don't interrupt. Let them work.

In parenting moments:

- **Give freedom within structure:** "You may choose your clothes, but they need to be appropriate for the weather."
- **Stay consistent with boundaries:** If you say clean-up comes before snack, hold that boundary lovingly.
- **Invite participation:** "You can help me fold the laundry or sweep the floor. Which would you like to do today?"

The goal is not control—it's collaboration.

Missteps and Misunderstandings

Most new Montessori parents veer too far in one direction, whether by allowing too much freedom or providing too much structure.

The overcorrected freedom approach is when you let your child lead everything based on momentary interests. There's no rhythm, no accountability, and no guidance. Eventually, you feel like things are slipping.

The overcorrected structure approach is when you try to do Montessori by-the-book. You stick rigidly to lesson sequences and start micromanaging the work cycle. Your child resists, and it doesn't feel joyful.

Instead, embrace the Montessori way. Freedom within limits means choice with accountability. Structure with flexibility. Leadership with humility. It means you give your children what they *can* handle—and nothing more than that. It evolves as they grow.

Practical Strategies to Get Started

Consider these practical tips to avoid overcorrecting in either direction:

- **Use clear language:** "This work is for your hands. Not for throwing."
- **Create rhythms, not rigid schedules:** Think flow and a predictable order to the day, not timestamps.

- **Adjust limits as needed:** Too much freedom? Rein it in. Too much structure? Loosen up.
- **Reflect often:** Ask yourself, *Am I setting a limit because it serves the child? Or because it comforts me?*

What Comes Next

Freedom within limits is the real answer to the question: *How do I follow the child as their leader?* It's the key to balance.

It allows your child to grow into independence without being thrown into the deep end. It empowers them with trust, while anchoring them with consistency. It honors their autonomy, while understanding their development.

And for you, the prepared adult, it's a tool that offers both clarity and calm—and allows you to respect your own knowledge, education, and capabilities. Because that matters, too. You have insights about how life works that your child doesn't yet. It is your responsibility to be their eyes in areas they cannot yet see.

Children do not build themselves from nothing. While learning is natural, it stems from experience—and it's your job to prepare that experience. The environment is not just physical. It is social and emotional as well. And Montessori teaches us that *the environment educates.*

Freedom within limits is how you take responsibility for shaping that environment. And who you become—your values, your habits, your beliefs—are shaped by it. The personality is largely formed in the first five years. Values take root in the habits you model, the boundaries you set, and the respect you show.

You don't have to choose between structure and child-led learning. Montessori gives you both.

Thoughts from the Frontlines

Hear how real families shifted their mindset, regulated their presence, and discovered how preparing themselves changed everything in their homeschool.

Mae-Lin: Army veteran and mother of one

"I thought the hardest part would be the lessons or the materials. But it was me. My mindset. My triggers. I had to regulate my nervous system before I could lead with calm, before I could hold space. I tell myself daily:'I'm a work in progress—and so is she'. That's Montessori."

Fatema: Former engineer and homeschooling mom of two in Saudi Arabia

"My biggest fear was me—my discipline, my ability to follow through. But I kept coming back to my 'why' and that kept me grounded. I started putting systems in place not just for my child's learning, but for *my* preparation. That's when it all began to shift."

Viviana: Doctor of nursing practice turned stay-at-home mom of three

"I used to think homeschooling was about getting everything right for my daughter. But I've learned it's also about healing myself. Through observation and reflection, I realized I was passing on pressure, not presence. Now I check in with myself first—because I set the tone."

Wilka: Multicultural mom of one

"In our first year, I was treating Montessori like a checklist. It wasn't until I began working on myself—my mindset, my tone, my trust in the process—that things started to click. I had to stop rushing and start *observing*. The prepared adult is not perfect. She's aware."

Tiffany: Colombian-American mom of three

"The hardest thing was just believing I could *do* this. Not because I didn't care, but because I was juggling so much. What helped most was learning that preparation isn't just about the shelves—it's about preparing *myself* to show up with calm, with clarity, and with flexibility."

To learn more about the families featured throughout this book, you'll find their bios in the appendix.

10

Understanding Montessori's Developmental Stages

Sensitive Periods and Planes of Development

If you've ever watched your child become completely absorbed in something—lining up animals, pouring water back and forth, scribbling the same mark over and over—it might have seemed random. But in Montessori, we ask a different question: *What developmental need is being met here?*

This is what it really means to follow the child—not to chase their every interest, but to learn how to observe what's happening beneath the surface. Why this activity? Why now? What part of their development is calling for this kind of work?

When you follow the child through this lens, you move from reacting to whims to responding with intention. And the best way to do that is by understanding how children grow.

What Montessori Means by Development

Montessori education is not based on age alone—it's based on *human development*. That includes how children think, what they're capable of, and what their brains and bodies are wired to do at different stages.

Montessori observed that development happens in *four distinct planes,* each with its own unique needs and characteristics. And within those planes, children experience *sensitive periods*—windows of time when they are biologically primed to master specific skills with ease.

This approach is one of the most important ways Montessori meets the child where they are. It's also why it works so well.

The Four Planes of Development

Montessori divided child development into four six-year cycles. Think of them as the developmental equivalents of seasons—each one with its own rhythm, mood, and priorities.

First Plane (0–6 years): The Absorbent Mind

This first plane is characterized by the following:

- Learning through all five senses
- Rapid language acquisition
- Deep need for order and consistency
- Sensitive periods for movement, language, and practical life
- Concrete, hands-on learning

Your role: Create a home that supports independence, routine, and repetition. Allow plenty of time for movement and exploration. Focus on real-world activities your child can do themselves.

Second Plane (6–12 years): The Reasoning Mind

This second plane is characterized by the following:

- Shift from concrete to abstract thinking
- Intense curiosity about the world
- Strong sense of justice and fairness
- Social expansion and group belonging

Your role: Feed their curiosity with stories, big questions, and open-ended projects. Support their desire for independence by giving them responsibilities and opportunities for collaboration.

Third Plane (12–18 years): The Social Self

The third plane is characterized by the following:

- Identity formation and emotional development
- Desire for autonomy and real-world experience
- Sensitivity to social belonging and meaning

Your role: Provide guidance without micromanaging. Offer real responsibilities. Make space for reflection, conversation, and contribution to the community.

Fourth Plane (18–24 years): The Mature Self

The final plane is characterized by the following:

- Self-direction and specialization
- Purpose-driven learning
- Drive to contribute to the larger world

Your role: Trust their autonomy. Encourage mentorship, continued exploration, and responsibility. Be available as a sounding board, not a manager.

Each plane builds on the one before. When you support the child appropriately in each stage, they grow into confident, capable adults who trust themselves and love learning.

Sensitive Periods: Nature's Built-In Learning Windows

Have you ever seen your child become laser-focused on something—pouring water back and forth for 20 minutes, stacking blocks with precision, or endlessly practicing a new word? It may seem random, but Montessori shows us there's something deeper happening.

These are signs of a *sensitive period*—a developmental window when the brain is especially primed to learn a specific skill. During this time, the child doesn't just want to learn—they *must*. It's a biological drive.

And when you respond with the right materials, enough time, and a prepared environment? They learn almost effortlessly.

During these sensitive periods, children:

- Gravitate toward certain activities or themes
- Repeat tasks with focus and determination
- Master skills quickly and joyfully

As Dr. Maria Montessori said, "A child's work is to create the person they will become." Sensitive periods are the blueprint for that creation. They're short, but powerful—and once they pass, learning that same skill later will still be possible, but it won't come as naturally.

Here are some common examples from the first plane (birth–6), when sensitive periods are most intense:

- **Language (birth–6):** Soaking up vocabulary, sentence structure, and grammar just by being immersed in it
- **Order (18 months–4):** Craving predictability, routines, and everything in its place
- **Movement (birth–4):** Refining gross and fine motor skills through repetition
- **Small objects (1–4):** An intense fascination with detail, precision, and tiny things
- **Social behavior (2.5–6):** Practicing grace, courtesy, cooperation, and empathy

These aren't just preferences—they're windows of opportunity. When you meet your child's sensitive period with respect and preparation, you give them tools for life.

And that's why the Montessori approach works so well: it's not built on arbitrary schedules. It's built on *developmental readiness*. Montessori meets the child where they are—when they're ready—not where a system says they should be. Figure 10.1 shows the sensitive periods in the first plane of development, ages 0–6.

Here are some common examples from the second plane: childhood (6–12 years):

- **Imagination and abstract thinking:** A shift from concrete experiences to conceptual exploration, allowing for storytelling, reasoning, and creative problem-solving.
- **Moral development:** A heightened awareness of fairness, justice, and ethical reasoning.
- **Group belonging and collaboration:** A strong drive to work in teams, form peer relationships, and establish social norms.

Here are some common examples from the third plane: adolescence (12–18 years):

- **Identity and Independence:** A deep search for personal meaning, purpose, and autonomy.
- **Critical thinking and self-reflection:** Developing the ability to analyze, question, and form personal beliefs.

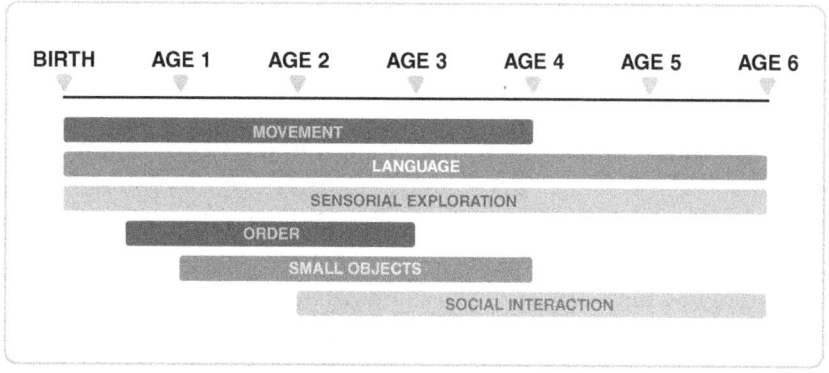

Figure 10.1   Sensitive Periods for the First Plane of Development.

- **Social justice and idealism:** A heightened awareness of societal issues and a desire to make an impact.
- **Real-world application:** A need for hands-on, experiential learning through apprenticeships, entrepreneurship, and life skills development.

How This Helps at Home

Understanding these stages doesn't mean you have to be an expert in child psychology. It simply means you start seeing behavior as *communication*.

- When your toddler insists on doing everything themselves—they're working on independence.
- When your six-year-old won't stop asking why—they're building reasoning.
- When your teen questions everything—they're forming identity.

When you know what stage your child is in, you can:

- Set more effective boundaries
- Offer the right kind of freedom
- Choose materials and activities that match their needs
- Let go of unrealistic expectations that create stress for both of you

This is how freedom within limits starts to make sense. Because development gives you the context for knowing *which* freedoms to offer and *which* limits to hold.

Montessori Meets the Child Where They Are

In traditional education, children are often expected to conform to standardized benchmarks. But in Montessori, we trust that children are already built for growth. Our job is not to push them toward outcomes—it's to *remove obstacles* so their development can unfold.

That's why this chapter matters so much. Because once you understand *how* children grow, you stop asking, "Am I doing this right?" and start asking, "What does my child need from me right now?"

That shift—from pressure to partnership—is what makes Montessori homeschooling so powerful.

What Comes Next

In Section 3, you'll take everything you've learned so far and bring it to life. You'll learn how to apply these principles practically: how to set up your space, observe your child, introduce lessons, and create a rhythm that works. This is where it all comes together.

Thoughts from the Frontlines

Montessori isn't about rushing to results—it's about recognizing readiness. Learn how real families came to understand development as a layered, nonlinear process and how learning to trust the planes and sensitive periods helped them step back and support their children more effectively.

Mae-Lin: U.S. Army veteran and trauma-informed parent
"I used to expect my daughter to 'get it' after one presentation. I had to relearn what mastery really means. When I understood how development works—how repetition and readiness show up differently in each child—I could finally slow down and meet her where she was. Not where I thought she *should* be."

Fatema: Stay-at-home Mom and mother of two in Saudi Arabia
"The three-year-old stage is a beautiful mix of independence and chaos. Understanding the planes of development helped me stop labeling things as 'regression'. Now I see it as recalibration. I respect the mess more—and myself more—for staying present through it."

(continued)

(continued)

Tiffany: Bilingual mom of three balancing biliteracy and Montessori
"I used to panic when my daughter wasn't reading as fast as someone else's kid. But learning about sensitive periods and the Four Planes helped me see the bigger picture. Development isn't a race—it's a rhythm. And every child hears it differently."

Wilka: Puerto Rican/Filipina mom of one, rethinking learning
"Once I stopped seeing learning as linear, everything shifted. My daughter was exploring complex ideas through pretend play, and I might've missed it if I only focused on 'output'. Montessori helped me observe *development*, not performance."

Maria Isabel: Colombian mom homeschooling in Sweden
"I used to get overwhelmed by the five curriculum areas. But when I studied the developmental stages, I realized it wasn't about 'covering it all'. It was about offering the right invitation at the right time. That changed everything about how I planned."

To learn more about the families featured throughout this book, you'll find their bios in the appendix.

3

Bringing It Home

Creating Montessori-Aligned Spaces, Rhythm, and Learning Environment

You've done the inner work. You've examined your beliefs, prepared your mindset, and grounded yourself in what matters most. You understand that Montessori isn't just about what happens at the shelf—it's about how your child experiences life, learning, and growth through an intentional environment and a prepared guide.

Now it's time to bring the philosophy into action.

This section is where you take everything you've learned and begin to *build*—not just a homeschool plan, but a way of living and learning that honors your child's development and works for your real life.

In the chapters ahead, you'll learn about the five essential elements of your Montessori homeschool foundation:

- **A home that teaches:** How to prepare your home as a whole—not just a classroom corner—so your child is included, respected, and supported in becoming self-disciplined, self-aware, and self-directed.

- **The Montessori learning space:** How to create a functional, focused, and beautiful learning space using what you already have—without needing a playroom or a Pinterest-worthy shelf.
- **The Montessori curriculum for homeschoolers:** What curriculum really means in Montessori, how to use albums and scope and sequence with intention, and how to choose resources that empower (not overwhelm) your role as guide.
- **Montessori materials:** What's essential, what can wait, what you can DIY, and how to make smart, aligned choices that support your child's development—not your fear of missing out.
- **Daily rhythm and flow:** How to craft a flexible, dependable daily rhythm that makes space for deep work, rest, movement, connection, and family life—without re-creating a school schedule.

This is the part many homeschoolers rush into: buying materials, setting up shelves, making schedules. But when you build on a strong foundation, your choices become clearer. You don't have to do everything at once. You don't need to replicate a classroom. You just need to begin—with presence, purpose, and patience.

By the end of this section, you'll be able to confidently say: *We're not just learning about Montessori—we're living it.*

Let's begin.

11

The Home That Teaches

Living the Method
Beyond the Shelf

Before we talk about shelf work, lessons, or materials, we have to talk about the space where all of that is going to live: your home.

Because no matter how beautifully your learning corner is organized, if the rest of the home environment is disjointed, disordered, or working against the child's development, then the learning won't stick. Montessori education isn't just what happens on the shelf—it's what happens in the child's life. And that life unfolds, first and foremost, in your home.

This chapter is about seeing your home as the first and most enduring prepared environment—not just a backdrop, but a foundation. Not a classroom, not a child-run kingdom, but a living, breathing family space where the child is considered, respected, and included.

Montessori Parenting Is Still Parenting

Even though this book focuses on education, you cannot separate Montessori homeschooling from the parenting work that surrounds it. You can't expect self-regulation and independence in schoolwork if the rest of the home is chaotic, reactive, or centered on adult convenience.

Montessori doesn't mean child-led chaos. It means shared purpose. Children are part of the family, not the center of it. They have a place and a voice, but they're also held by the structure and values of the family system. Parent with clarity, kindness, and consistency—not through control, but through example. That's grace and courtesy in action. That's real leadership.

When your child lives in an environment that models self-respect, mutual care, responsibility, and rhythm, those qualities become internalized. And that's the goal—not just academic achievement, but personal actualization. Montessori called this the *cosmic task:* the unique contribution a person brings into the world when they are supported in becoming fully themselves. Your home is where that begins.

Montessori Begins at Home

In traditional school settings, a child often exists in two very separate worlds: home and school. Montessori doesn't separate those spheres. It sees the child as a whole person and education as a whole-life process. That's why one of the greatest indicators of success in homeschooling isn't a full curriculum or a perfectly executed lesson—it's a home environment that supports the child's development.

So what does that mean?

It means the child is included—not centered, not indulged, but included. Their needs are considered in how the home functions, not just where their toys or schoolwork live. They have routines, responsibilities, a sense of place, and a sense of belonging. They're given time and space to become self-directed, self-organized, and—over time—self-disciplined. That's the real work of Montessori.

Before You Begin: Decluttering as a Montessori Practice

One of the most powerful ways to prepare your home for learning is also one of the most overlooked: *clearing the clutter.*

Montessori environments are intentionally simple—not for aesthetic reasons, but to reduce cognitive overload and promote deep concentration. The more a child has to sift through to find what they need, the more they're pulled out of focus.

That doesn't mean your home needs to be sparse or sterile. It means everything present should have a clear purpose. It should be usable, beautiful, and appropriate for this stage of your child's development. Before you rearrange furniture or plan shelf work, take time to *edit*.

Here's a Montessori-inspired decluttering approach, adapted from Marie Kondo's principles[1] with a Montessori lens:

- **Declutter by Category, Not Location**

  Start with one type of item—like toys, clothes, or books—not one room. This helps you see what you have in total and make more thoughtful decisions.

- **Hold Each Item and Ask: "Does this support my child's development?"**

  This is the Montessori version of "Does this spark joy?" If it's broken, too complex, too babyish, or rarely used, consider donating or storing it.

- **Involve Your Child**

  Even toddlers can choose which toys they use most or help organize their clothes. This fosters ownership and reinforces respect for the space.

- **Give Everything a Home**

  Children thrive when they know where things go. Clear trays, labeled bins, and accessible shelves support independence and ease.

- **Start with One Area—And Build from There**

  You don't need to overhaul your whole house in one weekend. Begin with the area your child spends the most time in. Let that transformation motivate the next.

Decluttering isn't a one-time event—it's a mindset. As your child grows, their needs evolve. So will your space. Let this process be a marker: you're entering a new chapter, and your home is growing with you.

Why Spaces Matter: Defining Function and Purpose in the Home

Before you get to arranging shelves or materials, step back and consider your home as a whole. Montessori environments are intentional. Every space in your home should support the life that happens there. This means clearly defining the purpose of each area and making sure the environment reflects that purpose.

Ask yourself:

- What happens in this space?
- Does everything here support that function?
- Can my child access what they need independently?

This could look like:

- The kitchen: Dishes, cups, and tools are within the child's reach so they can help with meals or clean-up.
- The living room: Books and cozy reading areas are available for quiet rest or storytelling.
- The bathroom: Toiletries and towels are accessible with a step stool.

The goal is not to create a child-centric home, but a child-inclusive one—where the child is considered as a contributing member of the family.

Integration, Not Imitation

One common misunderstanding in Montessori homeschooling is the idea that we need to build a miniature world just for the child—tiny kitchens, tiny tables, even tiny brooms and pretend food. But at home, your child doesn't need a parallel life. They need a meaningful role in the real one.

Children want to do what you do. And when we adapt our real spaces to allow that, something powerful happens: they rise to the occasion.

Instead of duplicating adult spaces, focus on integrating your child into real life:

- In the kitchen: Store dishes and tools where your child can reach them. A stool and a low shelf might be all that's needed.

- In the bathroom: Provide a step stool so they can wash their hands or brush their teeth independently.
- In the dining area: Invite them to help set and clear the table with real plates and utensils.

Dr. Maria Montessori believed that children should be included in real life—not separated from it. That's why a Montessori classroom imitates the home—not the other way around. A Montessori home invites participation. Children don't need a parallel world—they need real access to ours.

When you shift from creating a child-sized replica to making your home more inclusive, you're not just rearranging furniture. You're shifting the culture of your home. You're saying: You belong here. You're capable. You're needed.

Accessible vs. Prepared (in the Home)

In Montessori, accessibility and preparedness go hand in hand. But they're not the same.

Accessibility means everything your child needs is within reach—physically and developmentally. It's the practical setup: Can your child reach the materials? Are the tools sized for their hands? Can they carry the tray and complete the task without needing help every step of the way?

In the home, this might look like:

- Storing cups and pitchers on a low shelf so your child can pour their own water
- Hanging coats on a hook at their height
- Placing laundry baskets or step stools where they can help with chores

Preparedness, in the broader home context, means creating environments where:

- Expectations are clear and modeled consistently
- The child can participate meaningfully in real routines
- There's space for practice and refinement without correction at every turn

This isn't just about materials—it's about culture. A home that is both accessible and prepared is one that trusts the child's capability and offers them real opportunities to grow.

Practical Tips for Keeping It Real (and Real Montessori)

Montessori doesn't require perfection or performance—it requires presence, consistency, and a willingness to stay curious.

So how do you make the method work in your real, imperfect, beautifully complex life? Here are a few ways to keep it grounded and aligned with Montessori principles—without losing your sanity or your sense of self in the process.

Start with Practical Life

These activities are the heartbeat of early Montessori—and they don't require specialized materials. Washing produce, sweeping the floor, watering plants, folding towels, or preparing a snack—all of these are valid and valuable learning experiences. Practical Life builds coordination, confidence, independence, and order. Start here and build outward.

Use Observation to Guide Your Choices—Not Trends

It's easy to be influenced by Instagram-worthy shelves or other people's routines. But your child is your curriculum. Watch how they engage. What draws them in? What do they avoid? What do they return to again and again? Let those observations lead your next steps—not the algorithm.

Establish Consistent Rhythms

Children thrive on rhythm. Whether it's a predictable work cycle, a daily walk, or a shared quiet time in the afternoon, rhythm creates the security that makes freedom possible. It's not about rigid scheduling—it's about creating a flow that supports focus and reduces resistance.

Educate Yourself Before You Invest in Everything Else

Before you buy new materials, invest in your understanding. Read the theory, study the albums, and learn how to give a three-period lesson. The better prepared you are, the more effective any material will be. When you understand the why behind the work, your guidance becomes intentional and responsive.

Let Go of the Aesthetic

Montessori isn't beige. It's not minimalist for the sake of minimalism. It's not defined by the type of wood on your shelf. A real Montessori environment is one where the child can focus, where materials are complete and inviting, and where everything has a clear purpose. Focus on function. If it's meaningful, simple, and accessible, it's Montessori.

Create Margin and Build Slowly

You don't need to do everything at once. Choose one area of focus each month—or even each season. Maybe this season, it's building a consistent morning rhythm. Maybe it's getting clear on the early math sequence. Whatever it is, do it deeply before you move on. Montessori is not about quantity—it's about depth.

What Comes Next

When you commit to Montessori, you're not just choosing an educational method. You're choosing a way of living—a way of seeing the child, of relating to yourself, and of structuring your home to serve something greater than convenience.

Yes, you'll make mistakes. Yes, your child will resist sometimes. But the goal isn't to create a perfect Montessori household. The goal is to create a life where the child can grow in independence, peace, curiosity, and contribution.

This chapter isn't asking you to do more. It's inviting you to do differently. To see your home as a place of learning—not through posters and workbooks, but through culture, rhythm, and relationship.

When the Montessori philosophy echoes through your home—not just your lessons—you'll notice something incredible:

Learning doesn't start when the shelf work begins. It starts the moment your child wakes up. And it never really stops.

Thoughts from the Frontlines

Real-life reflections on transforming the home into a living Montessori environment.

Viviana: Montessori homeschooling mother of three in a multicultural home, small business owner

"We have a dedicated room for homeschooling. It's still a work in progress, but it's become a sacred space in our home. The materials are not toys—we've made that distinction clear. That room is for learning and doing purposeful work, and we've built our rhythm around it. The girls know that when we enter, we treat the space and each other with care. My toddler has a corner with her own shelves, and even she

(continued)

(continued)

understands the energy of the room is different from the playroom. Outside the classroom, we've also made small shifts—things like placing their water cups where they can reach them or giving them a place to store their daily work. It's helped them take ownership of their space, and I notice they are calmer, more focused—even proud."

Sarah: Homeschooling mother of four on a hobby farm in the U.S.

"Our homeschool space is in the basement, and honestly, it's grown with us. When we started, it was one shelf and a table. Now it holds materials for multiple planes of development across language, math, geography, and more. It's not fancy, but it's thoughtfully prepared. I reset it every afternoon, not just for cleanliness but for clarity—so when the children come in the next morning, they're greeted with order. Even outside our homeschool room, the house reflects what we're learning. My son might take his book to the porch to read while his sister helps collect eggs. The home becomes the environment when you realize it's all learning—if you treat it that way."

Tiffany: Bilingual homeschooling mom of three raising global learners in the United States

"We actually homeschool in our master bedroom. It's the biggest space in the house, and rather than waiting for ideal conditions, we worked with what we had. One side is our classroom, the other is a toddler corner, and the materials rotate depending on where each child is developmentally. The way we signal the shift into learning mode is through environment and rhythm. Deep focus music plays. The girls know the energy shifts, even if we're in a bedroom. It's taught me that Montessori isn't about perfect rooms—it's about the intentionality behind them. The home doesn't just support the child's learning. It teaches them how to be in a space with respect, care, and confidence."

To learn more about the families featured throughout this book, you'll find their bios in the appendix.

Note

1. Kondo, Marie, *The Life-Changing Magic of Tidying Up: The Japanese Art of Decluttering and Organizing* (Ten Speed Press, 2014).

12

The Montessori Learning Space

How to Set Up Your First Montessori Environment

There's a common misconception that a Montessori home must look a certain way—neutral-toned shelves, wooden toys, and a perfectly curated aesthetic. But Montessori is not an interior design trend. It's a way of designing a space that supports a child's natural development, independence, curiosity, and ability to engage in meaningful, self-directed work.

> "Montessori is not about what your home looks like—it's about how it functions for your child."

Montessori homeschooling isn't about replicating a classroom or spending a fortune on materials. It's about creating an environment where your child can move, explore, focus, and learn independently—right in the heart of everyday life. This chapter helps you set up your first Montessori learning space in a way that's simple, purposeful, and personalized to your home.

Creating a Purposeful Montessori Learning Space

You don't need to start with perfect furniture or materials; Montessori doesn't start with the shelf—it starts with the child. Use what you have. Observe how your child moves through your home, and let that guide how you build your environment. The goal isn't perfection—it's intentionality.

Forget the Pinterest aesthetic. Your child doesn't need an Instagram-worthy setup. They don't need to be doing whatever it is you saw your favorite influencer doing with their child. Like you, they need clarity, simplicity, and an environment that supports independence and concentration. Start small—two, three- tier shelves, a few thrifted or repurposed trays and baskets, and a natural color (cream, tan, or beige) work rug. Choose a corner that feels calm and welcoming. Let the space evolve as you do.

As you prepare, it's easy to slip back into school-based mindsets. You might find yourself wondering, "Is this enough?" or "Should I be doing more?" When that happens, revisit Chapter 2 on letting go of traditional paradigms, and Chapter 8 on the prepared adult. This isn't about doing it all—it's about doing what matters, with purpose.

Montessori is a practice, not a performance. Be present. Observe. Adapt.

Choosing Where to Set Up Your Learning Environment

In Montessori, the environment is the teacher. That's why your learning space matters—it communicates expectations, supports focus, and helps the child orient themselves to the work.

Whenever possible, keep the learning space separate from the bedroom. Bedrooms serve many functions—rest, play, emotional regulation. Combining work with rest can lead to blurred boundaries, overstimulation, and reduced clarity about expectations. A play area in the bedroom is fine, but avoid combining formal work materials with play whenever possible.

If you must use a shared or multipurpose area, prioritize the living room over the bedroom. Living rooms and learning spaces serve similar functions: calm, communal engagement. You can structure the environment, so it communicates: *This is a space for purposeful activity.*

Great places to set up your learning area include:

- A corner of the living room
- A dining room or breakfast area
- A guest room or dedicated loft
- A portion of a hallway nook or underused space

If your learning space shares a room with a television or entertainment area, cover or cancel distractions during work time. A blanket, curtain, or simply turning off ambient noise goes a long way.

Having a dedicated workspace matters. Research in both child development and environmental psychology supports the idea that consistent spatial cues promote focus, self-regulation, and long-term memory. When children work in a designated space, they learn to associate that space with concentration and self-discipline—key outcomes of the Montessori educational approach.

If you're using a multipurpose space, use furniture intentionally to define boundaries. For example, position a couch back-to-back with a shelf to visually separate the living area from the learning area. Small visual cues like rugs, lighting, and furniture placement can signal transitions in purpose without needing an entirely separate room.

This is about teaching your child to respect time and space for focused work. We're raising self-directed learners. And that means the environment must communicate: *This is a place where learning happens.*

The Role of the Shelf

Shelves are central in a Montessori learning space, not because they look nice, but because they function like a silent guide. A well-prepared shelf is an invitation: *Choose your work. Focus. Finish. Return it when you're done.*

Unlike a toy box, a Montessori shelf offers:

- One activity per tray or basket
- Each activity complete and ready to use
- A curated number of materials, sequenced by skill

While many families begin with a cube organizer because of its availability and the way it's marketed as Montessori-friendly, it does have limitations. Trays often don't fit well, and the fixed compartments reduce flexibility. If possible, opt for adjustable, three-tier shelves in a neutral or white finish. These provide more vertical space, better visibility, and easier access for your child. They also grow with your setup and are an excellent opportunity to DIY!

Simplicity is kindness. Clutter overwhelms. Empty space is your friend. A clear, structured shelf supports the kind of decision-making, concentration, and independence that defines Montessori learning.

Build for Independence

Everything in your child's learning space should be designed to reduce the need for adult help:

- Everything has a home
- Tools for cleanup are accessible and child-sized
- Furniture supports movement and autonomy
- The rhythm of the day is predictable and respectful

You're creating a space that says:

- You are trusted
- You are capable
- You are welcome here

That's what a Montessori environment teaches. Without a word.

Setting Up Your First Shelves

When you're ready to set up your first shelf, focus on five foundational areas:

- Practical Life: Fine motor and procedural activities that build independence and promote concentration
- Transition Shelf: High-interest, familiar activities that help bridge the shift from traditional learning to Montessori work

- Language: Spoken language, pre-reading, phonics/reading, and writing activities
- Mathematics: Concrete materials that build number sense, quantity, and basic operations
- A Thematic Shelf: A rotating cultural unit (history, science, geography, or culture)

You might notice Sensorial is not listed here. While Sensorial is a core part of Montessori education and plays a vital role in developing the child's senses and intellect, it's not essential to include in the first phase of setting up. In these early months, your focus should be on building consistency, establishing rhythm, and helping your child orient to the new learning environment.

As you grow in your role and gain observational clarity, you can begin layering in Sensorial and other content areas with greater purpose and confidence—aligned with both your child's readiness and your own development as a prepared adult.

Why This Works

- Practical Life builds coordination, patience, responsibility, confidence, and focus.
- The transition shelf helps bridge and make connections with concepts or activities the child is familiar with, with new work cycle expectations to support the development of grace and courtesy.
- Language and math provide structure and support your own learning of the Montessori sequence and how your child engages with structured materials.
- A thematic shelf allows the adult to practice cross-curricular planning and get familiar with work variations and lesson extensions using inexpensive widely available resources like printables and blog-based units.

The initial setup is a *deschooling experiment*—a chance for you to gather information, reflect on your child's needs, and begin making informed, intentional decisions that honor Montessori without overwhelm.

An Overview of Montessori Subjects

Montessori Subjects in the Primary Years (Ages 3–6)

Montessori education is organized into five core areas for children ages 3–6. These subjects are deeply interconnected and develop over time. Some—like Practical Life and Language—take center stage early on. Others—like Sensorial or Culture—are layered in as the child is ready and as you, the guide, grow in confidence and skill.

This overview gives you a clear picture of what each area includes and how it contributes to your child's development:

Practical Life: Focuses on care of self, care of the environment, grace and courtesy, and control of movement. These activities lay the foundation for independence, coordination, concentration, and responsibility.

Examples:

- Pouring water from one pitcher to another
- Washing a table
- Buttoning, zipping, and folding clothes
- Preparing a snack or setting the table

Sensorial: Refines the senses and builds the child's ability to classify, compare, and make sense of the world. Each material isolates one quality (such as size or texture) and encourages exploration through repetition.

Examples:

- Pink Tower: Ten pink wooden cubes in graduating sizes that introduce dimension, sequencing, and visual discrimination
- Color Tablets: Small tablets for sorting and grading color by intensity and hue
- Sound Cylinders: Pairs of sealed cylinders filled with various materials to match by sound
- Rough and Smooth Boards: Textured boards to help the child discriminate and name tactile experiences

Language: Begins with spoken language, then moves to phonemic awareness, writing, and reading—always grounded in hands-on experiences and developmentally appropriate pacing.

Examples:

- Object-to-picture matching
- Sandpaper letters (tactile exploration of letter sounds)
- Moveable alphabet (building words with loose letters)
- Story sequencing and early phonetic readers

Mathematics: Montessori math begins with concrete materials to help children understand quantity, place value, and the decimal system. That's right—Montessori doesn't begin with memory work or math facts! Instead, we offer hands-on experiences that create a solid foundation for the abstract thinking that memory work and facts build upon later.

Examples:

- Number Rods: Red and blue rods representing quantity from 1–10, building number sequencing and comparison
- Spindle Boxes: Wooden boxes used to match numerals with actual quantities, reinforcing the concept of zero
- Golden Beads: Beads grouped into units, tens, hundreds, and thousands for hands-on exploration of place value and operations
- Bead Chains: Color-coded chains used to skip count and explore square and cube roots

Culture: Culture includes science, geography, history, art, and music. In the first plane of development (ages 3–6), these subjects are introduced largely through thematic units, real-world exploration, and sensorial experiences.

Examples:

- Puzzle Maps: Wooden maps that develop geography, spatial awareness, and fine motor skills
- Lifecycles of Animals/Parts of a Plant: Materials that explore biology through hands-on, visual storytelling
- Basic Land and Water Forms: Simple models that teach geographic vocabulary like island, lake, peninsula, and gulf
- Montessori-Inspired Continent Boxes: Collections of photos, artifacts, and miniatures representing different continents to spark curiosity and cultural understanding

Montessori Subjects in the Elementary years (Ages 6–12)

In the second plane of development, Montessori subjects evolve to support reasoning, imagination, and abstract thinking. Children are now capable of deeper exploration, collaborative projects, and personal responsibility.

History
- The Great Lessons: Five impressionistic stories that introduce the universe, life, language, math, and humans through awe and imagination
- Timelines: Visual tools for placing people, cultures, and events into historical context
- Fundamental Needs of Humans: A framework for understanding how people live across time and cultures

Geography
- Landform Models: Continued exploration of physical geography
- Mapping and Biomes: Study of regions, ecosystems, and climate zones
- Flags and Global Cultures: Research-based work on cultural identity and global citizenship

Zoology and Botany
- Classification Charts: Tools for sorting and understanding animal and plant kingdoms
- Anatomy and Ecosystems: Deeper investigation of how organisms function and relate to their environments
- The Six Kingdoms: Foundational biology lesson exploring the classification of all living things

Physical Science and Chemistry
- Hands-On Experiments: Inquiry-based learning about states of matter, magnetism, energy, and other foundational concepts
- Scientific Method: Introduction to observation, hypothesis, and experimentation

Geometry
- Formal Geometry Lessons: Built upon sensorial foundations, using tools like the geometric cabinet, angle constructor, and classification charts
- Terminology and Measurement: Naming parts, calculating perimeter, area, and understanding relationships

Self-Initiated Research and Follow-Up Work: Open-ended investigations that allow children to pursue interests sparked by lessons, often resulting in presentations, creative projects, or further reading.

Looking Ahead: Montessori in Adolescence (Ages 12+)

By adolescence, Montessori education becomes more structured—yet remains deeply rooted in self-direction, collaboration, and real-world application. This stage responds to the adolescent's need for purpose, contribution, and identity development.

Key characteristics of Montessori at this stage include:

- Greater use of textbooks, reference materials, and integrated studies
- Deepened project-based learning across disciplines
- Practical life shifts toward economic independence (entrepreneurship, internships, life skills)
- Emphasis on self-reflection, contribution, and responsibility in community life

While the form may look more "traditional" at a glance, the heart of Montessori remains: supporting the whole child, honoring their developmental stage, and empowering them to shape their place in the world.

What Comes Next

The next chapter explores the Montessori curriculum in greater depth—how subjects connect, how to sequence lessons, and how to use observation to guide your planning in a way that's developmentally aligned and truly personalized to your child.

Thoughts from the Frontlines

Real stories of adapting and designing home environments that support independence, focus, and peace.

(continued)

(continued)

Wilka: Montessori homeschooling mother of one, Puerto Rican/Filipino family

"We turned our daughter's old playroom into our main learning area. One shelf is now dedicated to reference materials like atlases and dictionaries. I invested in extra shelving and a comfortable floor chair so I could observe without hovering. We have clear subject labels and wicker baskets so everything has a place. I even added a plant and a cozy nook for reading to bring in that sense of beauty and calm. Our space isn't large, but it feels intentional. It communicates, 'This is your place to grow'. I used to think I needed a classroom. But now I know I just needed a space that invites focus and honors her autonomy."

Mae-Lin: Single mom, U.S. Army veteran, raising a four and a half-year-old with a trauma-informed Montessori approach

"I live in an apartment, so I had to get creative. I use IKEA Billy bookcases, and each one holds a strand of learning—math, language, sensorial, culture. Each shelf holds a sub-strand. There's a central rug and a small adjustable table pushed against the back of a sofa. The large window behind the shelves fills the space with light. Plants sit on the railing shelves, and we have soft music playing. The room doesn't look like a classroom—it looks like a lived-in, loved-in space where learning naturally happens. It's peaceful. That peace helps me regulate too, so I can show up as a grounded guide."

Wennie: Montessori homeschooling mom of two, registered nurse, living in a small apartment

"Space is tight in our apartment, but I was very intentional. I followed Lynda's advice and didn't set up the learning area in the kids' bedroom—I wanted to preserve that as a place for rest. I leaned heavily on the essential materials list to keep things minimal and focused. The learning space has only what's needed—nothing extra to distract. There's lots of natural light, and I keep it clutter-free. I've found that fewer materials mean more engagement. When everything has a place, and the space feels calm, my children settle into their work without prompting."

To learn more about the families featured throughout this book, you'll find their bios in the appendix.

13

The Montessori Curriculum for Homeschoolers

What It Is, What You Need, How It Works

If you've been Googling "Montessori homeschool curriculum," chances are you've found yourself knee-deep in open tabs, Instagram posts, free printables, and curriculum bundles—all claiming to be "Montessori-inspired." It can feel overwhelming.

So let's simplify.

This chapter will help you understand what the Montessori curriculum really is (and what it's not), what you actually need to get started, and how to confidently use these tools in your homeschool.

Start Where You Are

Let's normalize something: homeschoolers—like classroom teachers—begin Montessori as "inspired." And that's okay. The difference between Montessori-inspired and authentic practice is intention.

Starting with an introductory curriculum, unit study resource, or hands-on printable can be helpful. In fact, I recommend it. Hometessori, for example, is a strong beginner-friendly resource with step-by-step lesson support. It's a great place to start. It feels familiar and offers you a starting point when you're unsure of how Montessori flows.

But here's the truth: It's not the whole picture. These tools provide scaffolding as you begin, but they should serve as bridges—not destinations. You'll return to them again and again for ideas and support, but your long-term goal is to deepen your practice. To observe more, guide more, and shift into higher-fidelity Montessori.

We all start Montessori-inspired. Authenticity comes with time.

Understanding Montessori Manuals and Albums

Let's start with language: in Montessori, we don't use the word "curriculum" in the traditional sense. Instead, we use *manuals* and *albums*—these are guides for you, the adult, not worksheets for your child. Think of them like a car manual: you don't read it cover to cover before driving, but you do consult it when you need to understand how something works.

A Montessori album contains lesson presentations for each material and subject area. It includes:

- The purpose of the lesson (called the "direct aim")
- What skills the lesson prepares for in the future (the "indirect aim")
- A detailed, scripted presentation for the adult

But here's the key difference: Montessori albums are *non-linear*. The albums house lesson presentations, while the scope and sequence provide suggested order and timing. You determine readiness based on observation—not age or grade. You don't start on page one and move straight through to the end. Instead, you choose lessons based on what your child is ready for—what they're showing interest in, what skills they're developing, and where they're being drawn.

Example: Let's say your child is suddenly obsessed with pouring water at breakfast. You might check your Practical Life album to find the corresponding presentation for pouring. That becomes your next lesson—not because it's "next" in a sequence, but because you've observed that child is ready.

Montessori education flows from *observation, not prescription.*

Types of Montessori Curriculum Resources

There is no single official Montessori homeschool curriculum—and that's a good thing. It means you're not locked into a rigid formula. You get to build something that fits your child's development and your family's rhythm. But that freedom requires discernment.

Not all materials labeled "Montessori" are aligned with Montessori pedagogy.

Curriculum tools are just that—*tools.* They don't replace your role as a prepared adult. Having a curriculum doesn't make your homeschool Montessori. Using a curriculum *in partnership with observation and understanding of the philosophy*—that's what matters.

The following sections look at the types of resources available and how to use them.

Open-and-Go Programs   These programs are designed for simplicity and convenience. You open the binder or PDF, follow the steps, and check the box. This structure can be helpful when you're just getting started or need something to lean on during a busy season.

But here's the risk: They can train you to follow instructions instead of following your child.

Example: An open-and-go lesson might say, "Present the sandpaper letters A–C this week." But maybe your child already knows those sounds and is interested in blending. If you're not observing—just following— you'll hold them back.

Use these for: Building initial confidence and rhythm. Know they are a starting point—not the whole journey.

Pair with: An introductory course like Kickstart to Montessori Homeschool by The Montessori Teacher™.

Recommendation: Hometessori—simple, accessible, and familiar for beginners. But don't stop there. Use it as your launchpad, not your landing zone.

Plug-and-Play Resources   These include printables, Pinterest activities, workbooks, subscription boxes, or packaged thematic units. They often fall under the "Montessori-inspired" label—but this can be misleading.

Use these for: Enrichment or seasonal fun—not as your foundation. When evaluating these resources, ask yourself:

- Does this activity isolate one skill?
  It should. In Montessori, each material or activity isolates a single concept (e.g., size, sound, letter sound) to support clarity and focus. If an activity combines multiple skills at once—like cutting, writing, and coloring—it may overwhelm the child and dilute the learning.
- Is it concrete before abstract?
  It should be. Montessori begins with hands-on, real-world experiences before moving to abstract representations like pictures or symbols. If the activity is purely paper-based, ask yourself whether it builds on a prior hands-on experience or could be made more concrete through objects or actions.
- Is it rooted in real experiences, not fantasy?
  Montessori supports imagination through reality, especially in the early years. Choose activities grounded in the child's real world.
- Does it allow repetition and independence?
  Materials should be self-contained and available for repeated use without adult intervention. After each lesson, clearly communicate that the work is now available for independent repetition. Avoid vague expectations—don't play "guess what's in my head." Instead, offer a brief grace and courtesy lesson to model what repetition looks like and why practice matters. In Montessori, everything is a lesson—including how we return to work with purpose and care.

Example: A printable butterfly lifecycle activity may align beautifully with a cultural unit—if paired with observation, books, and time in nature. But cutting, gluing, and labeling alone isn't Montessori. The activity should support discovery, not decorate your shelf.

PRO TIP   If you found it on Pinterest and it looks more "cute" than purposeful, pause. Montessori isn't about visual appeal—it's about developmental alignment.

Standardized Curriculum Packages   These are comprehensive kits marketed to cover all subjects for the year—often with pre-written lesson plans, schedules, and assessments.

Use with caution: While the idea of a full program can be comforting, these packages are often designed for performance and efficiency, not authenticity and responsiveness.

Red flags:

- Worksheets used as busywork
- Pacing based on grade level rather than readiness
- Performance-focused language ("stay on track")
- Box-checking resources

Ask yourself: Does this program center your child's development—or adult convenience?

Important Note: Prewritten lesson plans, schedules, and assessments are not recommended at any point in your Montessori homeschool journey. Subscription kits like Lovevery or MontiKids—though inspired by Montessori—are best suited for the infant/toddler years. They are not designed for educational depth and should not replace intentional, child-led work in the early childhood or elementary years.

Teacher-Created Albums   These are lesson albums created by Montessori-trained educators and independent guides. While many are deeply knowledgeable, these albums are not part of an official training center.

Use these for: Practical, real-life guidance rooted in experience—but with discernment.

Examples:

- Montessori RD
- Montessori House
- Keys of the Universe
- The Montessori Teacher's Collective
- InfoMontessori.com (Free)
- Montessorialbum.com (Free)

TIP Some of these programs, like Montessori RD and Montessori House, break albums into age-based subcategories or sell lessons in bundles. While this can feel approachable, it may unintentionally train you to follow a scope by age rather than through observation. Also, be mindful of marketing. Some creators include extensions or extra lessons to cross-sell albums or promote their products.

Training Center Albums These are the most rigorous and reliable Montessori albums—written by or for official training centers. They follow the highest fidelity to Montessori principles.

Use these for: Deep understanding and high-integrity practice.

Access Note: These are typically only available through enrollment in formal training programs.

Examples:

- **AMI (Association Montessori Internationale)**—internationally respected and rigorous
- **AMS (American Montessori Society)**—widely recognized and well-established
- **CGMS (Center for Guided Montessori Studies)**—MACTE-accredited online training center
- **NAMC (North American Montessori Center)**—more accessible, but not MACTE-accredited
- **AIM Curriculum**—accessible to homeschoolers through The Montessori Teacher™

These albums offer consistency, depth, and developmentally aligned presentations. If you have access to them, use them.

PAIR WITH Training or coaching. Curriculum alone does not equip you to teach Montessori with integrity. Training center albums are written for those undergoing formal instruction. If you don't have access to a training program or don't desire to earn a credential for your career, seek mentorship or coaching to understand the deeper why behind the lessons and ensure alignment in practice.

Scope and Sequence in Montessori

You might be wondering: if the albums aren't linear, how do I know where we're going? That's where the *scope* and *sequence* comes in.

- **Scope** = What to teach (the content areas)
- **Sequence** = When to teach it (based on readiness, not grade level)

Think of the scope and sequence as your GPS—it gives you a map, but you still decide the route based on traffic, weather, and your starting point. It helps you zoom out, while observation helps you zoom in.

Many Montessori resources provide either a table of contents (which lists topics) or a scope and sequence (which shows developmental flow). They are not the same. You need both.

Free scope and sequence resources:

- Montessori Compass—an interactive online scope and sequence tool with progress tracking
- The Montessori Teacher™ Scope & Sequence—available to home-schoolers as part of The Montessori Teacher's coaching services

Formal training programs also include detailed scope and sequence charts integrated into their albums, such as:

- AMI (Association Montessori Internationale)
- AMS (American Montessori Society)
- CGMS (Center for Guided Montessori Studies)

Important Note: Some creators now sell scope and sequence documents as plug-and-play curricula, marketing it as a pacing guide or as a standardized curriculum, with premade lesson plans. While these may provide structure, they do not teach you how Montessori works. These tools should be used with discernment—as reference points, not as instruction manuals. They are not a replacement for your preparation as a guide.

From Inspired to Authentic: A Mindset Shift

One of the biggest shifts you'll make is moving from asking:

- "How do I make this more fun?" to
- "How do I prepare the conditions for deep engagement & concentration?"

The first approach centers on the adult. The second centers on the child.

Instead of asking, "How do I get them to finish the activity?" ask, "What might be missing from the setup that's causing friction?"

Instead of saying, "They're bored with the bead chains." ask, "Have I observed long enough to see whether they're mastering or plateauing?"

Montessori isn't about getting kids to perform. It's about setting up the space for discovery.

Keep observing. Keep refining. Keep growing.

Start Before You Feel Ready

Let this be your permission slip:

- Your first shelf setup is a draft.
- Your first lessons will feel awkward.
- Your child will ignore things you thought they'd love.

That doesn't mean you're doing it wrong. It means you're doing it. Montessori is a process of observing, preparing, testing, and adjusting. It's scientific, human, and deeply intuitive once you trust it.

Try This: Choose one lesson from your Practical Life album. Observe your child for signs of interest or readiness. Prepare the material simply and clearly. Present it slowly—with few words. Step back. Observe again.

That's Montessori.

What Comes Next

The Montessori curriculum is not a script. It's a living framework. Your job isn't to follow it blindly. It's to understand it deeply—and use it in service of the child. You're not behind. You're becoming. And that's the most Montessori thing of all.

Thoughts from the Frontlines

What curriculum really looks like in practice—and how real parents use it to follow their children, not just a checklist.

Sarah: Montessori homeschooling mother of four, small business co-owner, living on a hobby farm

"I started out using a traditional curriculum, treating Montessori materials like manipulatives. But it drained the joy out of learning—for both me and my son. I let go of the boxed curriculum when he was six. From there, I used Montessori Research and Development manuals, supplemented with Cultivating Dharma. Observation became my compass. With four kids at different levels, I've had to be very intentional: grouping lessons by subject, staggering presentations, and prepping everything the night before. I know now that curriculum isn't about checking boxes—it's about preparing myself so I can respond to where each of my children really are."

Tiffany: Colombian-American mother of three, raising bilingual daughters and homeschooling without a background in education

"I didn't come from an education background, so figuring out curriculum felt overwhelming. I tried courses and bundles but kept ending up with gaps. Eventually I invested in a full set of Montessori albums so I could stop hunting and start planning. I use the AIM albums for structure and DIY a lot of the extensions using Canva and Teachers Pay Teachers—especially for bilingual work. I remind myself that curriculum is a guide, not a script. The moment I started planning around what my daughter needed—rather than what I thought she 'should' be doing—everything shifted."

(continued)

(continued)

Mae-Lin: Single mom, veteran, and intentional co-learner

"At first, I obsessed over finding the perfect curriculum. I bought three different ones—some too scripted, some too vague—and still felt lost. The turning point was realizing that the Montessori Scope and Sequence *is* the curriculum. I started using Lynda's planning template and finally understood how to zoom out with the Monthly Overview before zooming into the Roadmap. It's still not easy. I have to regulate myself first, then I can even begin to look at what she's ready for. But now I know that the curriculum isn't on the shelf—it's in the relationship between me, the environment, and my daughter's unfolding needs."

To learn more about the families featured throughout this book, you'll find their bios in the appendix.

14

Montessori Materials

What You Really Need and Why It Matters

The first time I walked into a Montessori classroom, I felt both wonder and worry. There were shelves full of elegant wooden materials, beautifully arranged, each with a purpose. I remember thinking: *How am I ever going to re-create this at home?*

I felt an urge to start filling my online cart with bead chains, sandpaper letters, and everything else I had seen.

If you've felt that same sense of overwhelm, you're not alone. Many new Montessori homeschoolers believe that to "do it right," they need to own everything—the Pink Tower, the Binomial Cube, the Golden Beads, the Sandpaper Letters. The list feels endless.

But here's the truth:

"Montessori materials are not about having more. They're about doing more with less—when used intentionally."

This chapter helps you understand what Montessori materials are, how they're different from traditional learning tools, and how to make smart, intentional choices about what to invest in—so your home environment can work for you, not overwhelm you.

What Are Montessori Materials?

Montessori materials are not toys. And they're not traditional teacher aids either. They are scientifically designed tools that support learning through hands-on, sensory-rich experiences.

Each Montessori material is created with a few essential design principles:

- **Isolation of a single concept** (e.g., just weight, just color, just size)
- **Built-in control of error** so the child can self-correct
- **Sequential complexity along the scope and sequence** from concrete to abstract
- **Repetition and mastery**

Examples:

- The *Golden Beads* let children hold units, tens, hundreds, and thousands in their hands. They don't just see the number 1,000—they *feel* it.
- The *Binomial Cube* looks like a puzzle but secretly introduces early algebraic thinking.
- The *Moveable Alphabet* allows children to build words long before they can hold a pencil—separating phonics from handwriting.

Compare that with traditional manipulatives like flashcards or counting bears, which often rely on adult instruction and don't encourage independent discovery. In Montessori, *the material is the teacher—the material is the lesson.*

DIY or Buy? How to Make Smart Material Choices

You'll hear a lot about DIY Montessori—and yes, some materials can absolutely be re-created affordably and effectively. For example:

- **Three-part cards** can be printed at home using free or paid downloads.

- **Practical Life trays** are often made with items you already own: a small sponge, a tiny pitcher, a child-sized spoon.
- **Sorting activities** can be created with dry beans, buttons, or seashells.

But for core math and language materials—like the Golden Beads or Sandpaper Letters—*precision matters*. Slight differences in size, texture, or color can confuse the child and interrupt the learning process.

RULE OF THUMB DIY the environment. Invest in the essentials.

Prioritize your spending on the materials that support foundational concepts. Think of them as an investment in long-term understanding, not just shelf aesthetics.

If your budget is tight:

- **Buy second-hand:** On Facebook Marketplace, Montessori resale groups, or homeschool co-ops.
- **Wait and observe:** You don't need everything at once. Introduce materials gradually.
- **Invest in your own education first:** Knowing what the material is for helps you decide whether it's even necessary for your child right now.

Investing in Your Own Education First

Before you buy a single material, invest in your ability to use it. Montessori materials only work when they're presented correctly—with the right intention, at the right time. Dr. Maria Montessori said:

"The first thing required of a teacher is that he be rightly disposed for his task."

When you're first getting started, this means:

- Learning how each material fits into your child's developmental stage
- Knowing how to use the material through an album or trusted training source
- Observing your child to decide what they need—not based on age, but based on readiness

A trained eye and a prepared mindset are more powerful than any object on your shelf. Consider:

- **Studying Montessori albums (manuals for presenting lessons):** Options include teacher-created albums like Montessori RD and Keys of the Universe, or albums available through training centers such as AMI (Association Montessori Internationale), AMS (American Montessori Society), and AIM (accessible via The Montessori Teacher™).

- **Watching video demonstrations:** Look for certified guides on YouTube, or explore video platforms like MontessoriTube, Educational Video Publishing, the AIM Video Lesson Subscription (available via The Montessori Teacher™), or The Montessori Teacher™ Home Learning Library, which provides video-based instruction.

- **Attending short online workshops or conferences:** The Childhood Potential Online Conference (offered twice a year) is a strong starting point and includes a membership hub for families in the first plane. Trillium Montessori provides workshops originally designed for classrooms that can be adapted to homeschool. The Montessori Teacher™ Home Learning Library also hosts practical workshops and mini-courses from home educators and Montessori guides around the world.

- **Hiring a Montessori coach:** A coach helps you grow your understanding, build sustainable systems, and tailor your approach to your child. I offer one-on-one support through The Montessori Teacher™, but others are available. Just make sure to clarify for yourself—not just how they market themselves—whether someone is a coach (focused on systems and strategy), a consultant (focused on offering advice), or a mentor (focused on sharing personal experience).

- **Joining a supportive community:** Look for communities where you can ask questions in real-time and get honest feedback. Options include The Montessori Teacher's Mighty Montessori Community and lifetime Montessori clinics, the Childhood Potential hub, Angela Montessori's live Zoom Q&As, and Montessori-focused homeschool groups on Facebook or Mighty Networks. A quick search for "Montessori homeschool" will yield many active forums.

This preparation will help you avoid overwhelm, wasteful purchases, and ineffective shelf work. The goal is not to mimic a classroom—it's to meet your child where they are.

A Note on Formal Training

Formal Montessori teacher training is not necessary for homeschoolers unless you have career aspirations in a specific age group. Training programs are typically:

- Focused on one age group (e.g., 0–3, 3–6, 6–12)
- Designed for classroom educators
- Time-intensive and often include student teaching or practicum requirements

Even programs like NAMC (North American Montessori Center), which are not MACTE-accredited, follow a classroom-centered model. Most training emphasizes lesson demonstrations, manual study, and documentation—all of which can be accessed in more flexible formats by homeschoolers.

You don't need to know everything about everything. The systems you create and your familiarity with how Montessori works matter most. Authentic practice starts with preparation—not perfection.

What You Actually Need to Start (and What Can Wait)

Montessori classrooms contain hundreds of materials—but your home doesn't have to. This section breaks down what's most essential for home-schoolers. My recommendations here are based on materials that introduce foundational topics (must-dos to follow the Montessori scope and sequence) or can be repurposed to create other Montessori lessons.

As a homeschooler, you'll likely be using one material per child. That means you can prioritize depth and intentionality over quantity. Certain materials can also be repurposed, giving you more value while still upholding the integrity of the Montessori approach. This is how we remain both faithful to the method and mindful of budget.

NOTE The age range listed represents the typical range of use. For example, a child will receive multiple lessons using the golden beads from around age 4 through age 7. That's right—you'll keep coming back to this material for 3+ years.

Essential Materials

Math

- **Golden Beads (ages 4–7):** For building foundational place value understanding
- **Stamp Game (ages 4–9):** For introducing dynamic operations with abstraction
- **Decanomial Box (ages 4–12):** For early counting, addition, and intro to multiplication. The most colored beads you'll ever use in one lesson is the decanomial lesson. As a homeschooler, you can purchase this box to recreate other colored bead lessons like the short bead stair or the snake game.

Language

- **Sandpaper Letters (ages 3–4):** For phonemic awareness and letter sound association
- **Moveable Alphabet (ages 4–6):** For building words before writing
- **Metal Insets (ages 4–6):** For building pencil control and hand strength
- **Function of Words/Grammar Boxes (ages 6–9):** For exploring parts of speech through hands-on classification

Sensorial/Geometry

- **Geometric Cabinet (ages 3–9):** For shape recognition and pre-geometry
- **Constructive Triangles (ages 4–9):** For discovering how shapes combine
- **Box of Sticks (ages 6–12):** For measuring, labeling angles, and building shapes

---

Cultural

- **Large Continent Puzzle Map (ages 4–7):** For early geography and cultural connections to History, Science, and Unit Studies
- **Timeline of Life (ages 6–12):** For understanding biological history and classification

Nice-to-haves (you can add later):

- **Pink Tower, Brown Stair (ages 3–4):** For visual discrimination and sequencing
- **Montessori Bells (ages 4–9):** For auditory discrimination and pitch matching
- **Land and Water Forms (ages 4–6):** For geography and language enrichment
- **Botany/Zoology Puzzles (ages 4–7):** For parts of plant/animal study
- **Additional Timelines (ages 6–12):** For elementary cultural work

Where to Source Materials

Buy new:

- Alison's Montessori (Value Line)
- KidAdvance (skip sensorial)
- Adena Montessori (skip sensorial)
- International Montessori suppliers (like Nienhuis)

Buy secondhand:

- Facebook Marketplace
- Montessori resale groups
- Local homeschool groups
- eBay (search for known brands: Nienhuis, Gonzagarredi)

Avoid:

- Cheap knock-offs that look similar but lack precision
- "Montessori toys" made of plastic or marketed for play only
- Miniature sets or random bundles without scope

DIY smartly:

- Thrift stores are gold mines for bowls, pitchers, tongs, and so on
- Use real-life objects for sorting and transferring
- Print three-part cards from trusted Montessori creators

What's a Supplement and What's a Substitute?

Montessori supplements are tools that *support* the child's learning alongside the core sequence—but they don't replace it. Substitutes, on the other hand, *attempt to* mimic Montessori materials without following the full pedagogy, often losing depth, precision, or developmental alignment.

Supplements reinforce concepts you've already introduced through Montessori presentations. *Substitutes* replace the real materials without offering the same experience or purpose.

Examples of Montessori-aligned *supplements* include:

- *Treasures From Jennifer* wooden calendars
- *Waseca Biomes* maps and classification cards
- *Mirus Toys* boards for place value or parts of speech

These are beautiful, useful, and often more accessible—but they don't replace the core Montessori materials or presentations. Use them to *reinforce concepts*, not to *introduce new ones*.

What Comes Next

Here's the big takeaway. You don't need to own everything to "do Montessori." You need to understand what you own—and know when and why to use it.

Start here:

- Invest in your own learning before buying more
- Observe your child to guide your material choices
- Focus on depth over quantity: This means offering fewer materials but using them more intentionally. Rather than trying to cover every topic at once or display every possible lesson, concentrate on presenting a smaller number of high-value materials that support repeated, purposeful use. A single well-understood material that's returned to often is more beneficial than a shelf full of under-used options.

Because the best Montessori shelf isn't the fullest one. It's the one that supports real growth, nurtures curiosity, and invites the child to return again and again.

"Montessori at home works best not when you have *everything*—but when you understand the *why* behind everything you have."

Thoughts from the Frontlines

How real parents navigate the overwhelm of materials—and choose what matters most for their unique child and environment.

Viviana: Doctor of Nursing Practice turned full-time home-school mom of three, running a small business
"When I started, I bought materials I saw on Instagram—sandpaper letters, movable alphabet, golden beads. They were helpful, but I quickly realized that materials alone don't make it Montessori. I invested in the AIM albums so I wouldn't constantly feel unsure about what I was missing. I DIY extensions to save money—Canva is my best friend—and use Teachers Pay Teachers for printables aligned to the albums. But more than anything, I realized I needed to stop

(continued)

(continued)

obsessing about owning *everything*. What matters is how well I know my child and whether the material helps her take the next step, not how pretty it looks on the shelf."

Wennie: Nurse and part-time working mom of two, Montessori homeschooling in a small apartment

"Space is tight, so I had to be intentional. I followed Lynda's 'essential materials' guide and skipped the Pinterest rabbit hole. I focused on self-organization instead—my own time, systems, and how I rotate what's out. It helped me see that having fewer materials actually creates more clarity and calm. The key wasn't having every piece—it was learning *how* and *when* to use what we already had. And honestly, the freedom to let go of 'more is better' made me a better guide."

Wilka: Montessori homeschooler in a multilingual, working family household

"In our first year, I treated the materials like a checklist—and I was overwhelmed. I'd try to introduce everything because I thought that's what I was supposed to do. But then I realized that the materials are just a *means*—not the goal. I started asking: 'What's this for? Does it serve *her* right now?' That's when everything clicked. Now I prep a few key materials each term based on our scope and sequence, and we revisit work at different levels of depth. I still get excited about new things, but I ask myself if I'm buying it to serve her—or to soothe my own uncertainty."

To learn more about the families featured throughout this book, you'll find their bios in the appendix.

15

Creating a Daily Rhythm

The Balance Between Structure and Flexibility

When I first began homeschooling, I made the mistake many of us make: I tried to replicate school at home. I built a color-coded schedule that broke the day into tidy 30-minute segments—math from 9:00 to 9:30, language from 9:30 to 10:00, practical life from 10:00 to 10:30. On paper, it looked perfect.

In practice? It unraveled by lunch.

My child wasn't ready to stop working when the clock said to move on. Some activities went faster than I planned. Others took longer. And I felt like I was constantly managing the schedule instead of supporting the learning.

It took time, patience, and observation to realize that what we needed wasn't a rigid schedule—we needed a rhythm. A flow. Something predictable, yet flexible enough to support real learning.

Why Rhythm Matters More Than a Schedule

Montessori education thrives on consistency and autonomy. A daily rhythm offers both.

Unlike a strict schedule, a rhythm is the natural order of your day—anchored by recurring routines, but open enough to respond to your child's interests and developmental needs. It builds trust and helps children know what to expect, while leaving room for them to go deep into their work.

The foundation of your daily rhythm? The uninterrupted *three-hour work cycle*.

This time block is non-negotiable in Montessori education. It gives your child the time to choose work, explore it deeply, repeat it, and restore it—without being rushed. Everything else in your day can flex around this anchor.

The following sections walk you through step by step on how to establish this rhythm from Day 1.

Step 1: Define Your Core Values

Before you shape your homeschool rhythm, take a moment to reflect: What matters most to you—not just as a homeschooler, but as a family?

Are independence and self-motivation important to you? Do you value connection and family time? Do you crave peace, presence, simplicity, or flexibility?

Let those values guide how your days unfold. Rhythm isn't about fitting more in. It's about building a flow that aligns with your family's core truths.

For example:

- If *independence* is a value, include time for your child to make their own snack or care for their space.
- If *connection* matters, make shared mealtimes and read-alouds a protected anchor.
- If *presence* is your goal, build in transition moments that allow for calm, undistracted guidance.

These values become the foundation of your daily rhythm—not to-do list items, but guiding principles that keep you aligned.

Start by identifying six to eight core values you want your days to reflect. These aren't goals or ideals—they're your family's non-negotiables. Your reflection and implementation journal includes a value list to help you clarify and narrow your focus.

Step 2: Chunk Your Day and Prioritize a Three-Hour Work Cycle

Instead of mapping out every minute, divide your day into broad time blocks. Each one should have a clear expectation, not a rigid task list.

Here's an example of a Montessori-inspired daily rhythm:

Time Block	Purpose
Morning Routine	Wake-up, hygiene, breakfast, light movement
Work Cycle (Three Hours)	A mix of collaborative work and focused independence This includes: • Read-alouds, songs, journaling, or shared discussions • Adult-guided Montessori lessons • Independent repetition using Montessori materials • Practical life activities • Language and math work • Sensorial exploration • Cultural subjects like science, geography, and art This protected time fosters concentration, confidence, and self-direction. Children move through the work cycle at their own pace, guided by interest and readiness.

(continued)

(continued)

Time Block	Purpose
Lunch and Connection	Share a meal, read aloud, relax together
Outdoor/Practical Life Practice	Nature walk, free play, gardening, errands, food prep, and household tasks
Afternoon Quiet Time	Reading, puzzles, quiet shelf work, journaling, independent exploration
Family Dinner and Household Responsibilities	Cooking, cleaning, setting the table, connecting, conversation
Evening Routine and Bedtime	Storytime, reflection, hygiene, rest

Remember: The goal isn't to follow a rigid timeline—it's to create a predictable, calming rhythm that helps your child understand what comes next and what's expected.

> **NOTE** The three-hour work cycle doesn't mean constant activity or one lesson after another—this isn't a traditional classroom. A three-hour work cycle is a protected window for concentration and a dedicated time for study that shows the child that learning matters and forms the habit of study as priority. We are raising lifelong learners, after all. Children may flow between focused work and restlessness. Your role is to maintain a calm, prepared environment and protect that time from unnecessary interruptions. Take a deep breath and stay present. The work cycle is often much more about the adult's ability to stay present than it is about the child.

Step 3: Understand Expectations and Tasks

Many homeschoolers confuse these two concepts. Clarity here will change how you guide your child.

- *Expectations* are the purpose or goal of a time block.
- *Tasks* are the actions your child might take to fulfill that expectation.

Understanding this difference allows for flexibility within structure. The following charts clarify how this applies in a Montessori homeschool.

Expectations vs. Tasks: Morning Routine

Expectation	Tasks (Examples Based on Child's Age)
Wake up and begin the day with independence	• Toddler: Choose a morning outfit from two options • Child (3–6): Dress independently, brush teeth with supervision • Child (6+): Fully independent morning routine
Contribute to breakfast preparation	• Toddler: Help carry a napkin to the table • Child (3–6): Pour own drink, set silverware • Child (6+): Help cook a simple dish, serve others
Care for personal hygiene	• Toddler: Wash hands with guidance • Child (3–6): Brush hair and wash face • Child (6+): Independently manage grooming
Prepare the environment for learning	• Toddler: Help place a work mat • Child (3–6): Choose a workspace, prepare materials • Child (6+): Ensure workspace is tidy before starting work

When you define expectations, your child has a clear understanding of what needs to be done without unnecessary pressure.

Expectations vs. Tasks: Montessori Work Cycle

Expectation	Tasks (Examples Based on Child's Age)
Engage in independent work	• Toddler: Work for short periods, explore through movement • Child (3–6): Choose work from the shelf, repeat exercises • Child (6+): Follow a work plan, complete a sequence of lessons
Respect materials and restore them	• Toddler: Assist in putting items back • Child (3–6): Restore work before selecting another • Child (6+): Return work to its place and check for completeness

(continued)

(continued)

Expectation	Tasks (Examples Based on Child's Age)
Seek guidance appropriately	• Toddler: Signal for help with gestures • Child (3–6): Ask with words before frustration escalates • Child (6+): Use a help card or approach the guide calmly

When expectations are clear and consistent, children develop independence.

Step 4: Use Anchors to Support Transitions

Transitions can be hard for children. Anchors help signal when one part of the day is ending and another is beginning.

Using Anchors to Structure the Day

Natural Anchors	Artificial Anchors
Sunrise/waking up	A song that signals time to start a new activity.
Mealtimes	A routine phrase: "When we finish eating, we clear our dishes."
A parent's work break	A visual schedule.
Sibling naps	A transition object (e.g., a work mat rolled out to signal work time).

Start with one or two natural anchors and layer in artificial ones only as needed. Teach transitions slowly and model them consistently.

Step 5: Lead with Presence, Not Pressure

Presence is about showing up as the prepared adult—not hovering, but quietly anchoring the environment. Here are some habits that are tried and true:

■ Get ready before your child starts their day. This lets you offer silent guidance instead of reactive correction.

■ Create uncluttered spaces that communicate: *You are welcome here. You are capable. You are supported.*

■ Resist the urge to micromanage. Instead, use observation as your primary tool. Remove what's confusing and superfluous. Too many toys, overly complex setups, or materials requiring skills your child hasn't yet developed can all disrupt focus. For example, avoid placing a box activity on the shelf if your toddler hasn't yet mastered how to open it independently. Instead, offer work that allows them to build that skill gradually. Remember—Montessori materials should meet the child where they are.

The environment should never overwhelm the child. It should call them to purposeful activity and growth. Yes, there will be seasons of life when staying present is difficult—like when caring for an infant or recovering from illness. But often, it's our habits—not our circumstances—that dictate how we show up.

As James Clear said, "You do not rise to the level of your goals. You fall to the level of your systems."

Let your habits support your presence. Let your presence support your child.

What Comes Next

A daily rhythm isn't about squeezing productivity out of your child—it's about crafting a home culture that reflects your values, fosters independence, and honors the developmental needs of the child.

You are not just building a schedule. You are setting the tone for how learning, rest, and connection are experienced in your home.

This rhythm—centered around focus, calm, and collaboration—creates the conditions for deep work, meaningful rest, joyful connection, and personal growth—for both of you. And while the schedule may evolve with seasons, the culture you build will leave a lasting impact.

Montessori isn't just about how your home looks—it's about how it functions. It's not about fitting learning into your life; it's about designing a life where learning is lived.

You don't need a rigid plan or perfect shelf. What you need is rhythm, consistency, and presence.

Because as Montessori reminds us, it's not the materials that matter most. It's the mindset of the adult and the environment they prepare.

Let your daily rhythm reflect that truth.

Thoughts from the Frontlines

Real-life rhythms that blend structure with flexibility—how Montessori home-schoolers build flow, not just routines.

Sarah: Mother of four, balancing homeschooling with working and running a hobby farm

"Over the years, our rhythm has evolved, especially with a toddler in the mix. A typical day starts with group time—maybe scripture, a shared story, or a grace and courtesy lesson—then each child moves into their work plan. I rotate between giving lessons, observing, and helping with toddler needs. Our afternoons are flexible: errands, co-op, or just being outside. But the reset at the end of the school day is key—reorganizing materials, restoring the space, and preparing for tomorrow. That's what keeps everything flowing."

Mae-Lin: Former Army officer and trauma-informed homeschooling mom

"We don't run on a strict clock. We use music and natural anchors. My daughter chooses the music—Colombian, Mandarin, or piano—and that signals it's time for the work cycle. I set expectations in the morning about which 3–5 works we'll cover. Then I let her decide the order and we check in throughout. Snack is an anchor. Reset music is another. And in the afternoon, I schedule in my own regulation time—therapy, reflection, something that lets me come back to center. Without that, our rhythm breaks down."

Wennie: Nurse and Montessori homeschooler in a small apartment

"I don't use exact times. I block the day instead: morning is for getting ready, breakfast, and our three-hour work cycle. Appointments and classes are always in the afternoon. That keeps the morning sacred. I also use visual schedules and audio cues, like a bedtime playlist or an alert to signal transitions. As a nurse, I learned that rhythms don't have to be rigid—they just need to be consistent. When my kids know what to expect, they feel secure, even if the day shifts slightly."

To learn more about the families featured throughout this book, you'll find their bios in the appendix.

4

From Preparation to Practice

A Practical Guide to Beginning Your Montessori Homeschool Journey

You've done the inner work. You've had the hard conversations, examined your beliefs, clarified your values, and made the bold decision to homeschool. You've spent time learning the Montessori philosophy, preparing your environment, understanding the role of materials, and crafting a rhythm that supports both structure and freedom.

Now, comes the most common question: *How do you actually begin?*

This section is your answer.

Here, we move from preparation to practice. This is where Montessori shifts from theory to daily reality. Each chapter offers practical tools, examples, and step-by-step support to help you guide your child with confidence, clarity, and flexibility.

In this section, you learn how to:

- *Present your first Montessori lessons* without overwhelm or perfectionism
- *Know exactly what to do on Day 1, Week 1, and Month 1,* even if you're starting from scratch
- *Recognize and respond to early* roadblocks like resistance, doubt, or burnout
- *Support your child's emotional, social, and developmental needs* as they transition into a new learning rhythm
- *Use observation and repetition as tools* for growth, not just academic markers

This section is primarily written with children ages 3–9 in mind. That's the age range when foundational Montessori work occurs, and many families begin their homeschooling journey. If your child is starting Montessori later (age 9+), you'll still find this guidance relevant, but you may need to adapt certain recommendations. Older children often shift from hands-on materials to research, dialogue, project-based work. That shift is natural—and Montessori supports it.

You'll find notes throughout this section pointing out how to adjust the approach for older beginning learners.

Although Montessori lessons are often scripted to support your understanding of how to present a material, they are not meant to be delivered robotically or followed verbatim. These presentations are not formulas—they are guides. They help you visualize the flow of a lesson and understand its objective.

Montessori comes to life not through perfect delivery, but through rhythm, relationship, and responsiveness. After all, we follow the child. And what good is a perfect lesson if no one is listening?

That's why this section isn't just about *what* to teach—it's about *how* to guide.

You don't need to be fully ready to begin. The most important thing you bring to this next phase is your willingness to show up. To observe. To adapt. To begin the practice of trusting yourself as your child's guide.

By the end of this section, you won't just understand Montessori—you'll be living it. And you'll have the tools to move forward with presence, purpose, and peace of mind.

Let's begin this work of practice—together.

16

Introducing
Montessori Lessons

A Simple, Powerful Start

For many homeschooling parents, this chapter is the one they've been waiting for. The shelves are set up. The space is ready. You've studied the method, stocked up on a few materials, and maybe even practiced pouring water or tracing a sandpaper letter yourself. Now you're asking:

> "What do I actually do when I sit down with my child?"
> "How do I start teaching, the Montessori way?"

Let's start by getting one thing clear: Montessori doesn't treat lesson presentation like a performance. You are not a lecturer. You're not an entertainer. You're not a curriculum deliverer. Your job isn't to make a lesson "fun" or to ensure that your child is excited about every activity. You are not the keeper of all knowledge.

You're a *guide*. And your first job is to observe—genuinely observe—how your child interacts with the environment. Be curious about their reactions. Model how to think through problems, make decisions, and engage deeply. Support concentration. Set clear expectations and follow through. Hold space for emotional growth, responsibility, and the discomfort that can come with accountability—for yourself and your child.

This chapter offers more than lesson scripts. It offers;

- A *clear framework* for presenting your first Montessori lessons
- A practical way to begin with *confidence and clarity*
- And most importantly—a way to begin without sacrificing the soul of the method

If that sounds too simple, or if you're tempted to reach for a checklist instead—pause. You're building a foundation. One that makes deeper, truly personalized, lesson planning possible. Montessori doesn't rush to deliver—it prepares for discovery.

What a Montessori Lesson Is (and What It Isn't)

In traditional education, a lesson is often a download. The teacher tells, the child listens, and the outcome is measured by how well the child retained what was said. Montessori flips that model entirely.

In Montessori:

- The *material* teaches, not the adult.
- The child's *hands and senses* are the gateway to understanding.
- The lesson is not the goal—it's the *invitation*.

A Montessori lesson is a quiet, purposeful demonstration that introduces a material to the child *just enough* so they can explore it independently.

You guide by:

- Inviting the child in
- Modeling the steps with care
- Communicating expectations of work and behaviors clearly
- Explaining how they can return to this work on their own
- Offering the material as a choice for practice
- Stepping back and observing

And while this might feel almost *too* simple—it's profoundly intentional. The silence, the slowness, the hands-on engagement—these are all elements that support concentration and self-construction.

What Makes a Montessori Lesson Different?

In a traditional lesson, the adult talks. The child listens. In Montessori, the adult presents, and the child explores. The material is the teacher.

Montessori lessons are:

- **Concise:** Less talk, more action.
- **Hands-on:** The child engages physically, not just mentally.
- **Quiet:** Fewer words mean more concentration.
- **Intentional:** Each movement is deliberate and purposeful.

This may feel unfamiliar at first. That's okay. Just like your child, you're learning.

Why We Don't "Plan Lessons" the Traditional Way

Traditional lesson planning typically involves creating a daily or weekly schedule, aligning it to grade-level standards, and following a predetermined scope and sequence—regardless of the child's actual readiness. The adult often delivers content through lectures or scripted instruction, assigns follow-up tasks, and evaluates proficiency based on predetermined benchmarks. This system values uniformity, efficiency, and control over responsiveness, mastery, and intrinsic motivation.

Montessori is different. It's not a one-size-fits-all model, and that's intentional.

In Montessori:

- **The child, not the calendar, guides the sequence.** Lessons are introduced based on direct observation of interest and readiness—not arbitrary age or timelines. A well-constructed Montessori scope and sequence is not a checklist to complete, but a developmental road map that reflects the natural progression of materials as they align to the child's Sensitive Periods.

- **Presentations aren't one-and-done.** A child may revisit and repeat the same material for days or weeks as part of their process of learning and mastery.
- **Planning without observation is guessing.** Montessori guides don't plan based on assumptions, checklists, or external standards. We plan based on what we've observed and use that information to make intentional decisions to craft a personalized learning experience.
- **Scope and sequence align with human development.** Montessori presents concepts over three-year developmental cycles, much like high school or college, where broad learning goals are met flexibly across multiple years.
- **The materials follow developmental science.** Dr. Montessori developed her method by observing sensitive periods and developmental milestones. Understanding the *purpose* behind each material—and its place in the sequence—is key to effective implementation.

Important note: This doesn't mean you don't plan. You absolutely do—but you plan differently:

- You prepare yourself—your presence, patience, self-awareness, and responsiveness.
- You study child development and developmental sensitivities.
- You prepare the environment with the child in mind, curating every object in their space.

You stay one step ahead, but not 10—thoughtfully observing, preparing, and guiding based on what your child actually needs.

Give yourself grace. In time, you'll develop the kind of observational rhythm that allows for full Montessori planning. But first, you have to begin.

Start with Grace and Courtesy

Before you introduce academic materials, begin with grace and courtesy lessons.

These are not just manners or niceties. They are the foundation for peaceful learning and community life.

In traditional education, expectations are often stated as rules—and then enforced. But Montessori takes a different approach: we teach expectations through modeling and practice. We understand that internalization of values and habits takes time. We don't assume that because we've said something, the child will do it. We teach by doing. We teach by teaching—not by correcting.

As Dr. Montessori reminds us, "A child who becomes a master of his acts through long and repeated exercises. . . is a child filled with health and joy and remarkable for calmness and discipline."

We begin with what's practical and familiar—how to roll a mat, carry a tray, wait your turn, interrupt politely, ask for help, or walk around someone else's workspace. Grace and courtesy lessons are not one-size-fits-all and should reflect your family's values, home culture, and real-world needs. They can be taught responsively, as situations arise, or proactively, based on patterns you observe.

Many new Montessorians equate Montessori with freedom and misinterpret that to mean letting the child do whatever they want. But self-direction is an outcome—not a starting point. As Dr. Montessori said, "To let the child do as he likes when he has not yet developed any powers of control is to betray the idea of freedom."

Grace and courtesy is the bridge to that control. These lessons create the environment where concentration, cooperation, and responsibility can grow.

Teach one skill at a time. Model it with the same clarity and care you'd bring to a math or language lesson. Reinforce the lessons through real-life application—both during your learning time and throughout the day.

Montessori homeschooling is a lifestyle. Grace and courtesy ties it all together.

In Montessori, education is a work of self-organization. That begins here.

The Three-Period Lesson: A Core Montessori Tool

The three-period lesson is a foundational Montessori strategy for vocabulary acquisition and concept development. Originally developed by French educator Édouard Séguin, this method supports deep learning through repetition, recognition, and recall. You'll use this structure across subject areas—not just for Montessori materials like the sandpaper letters or color tablets, but also for complementary curriculum extensions that align with Montessori philosophy.

Period One: Naming—"This is. . ."

- Present one item at a time and name it clearly.
- For example, with sandpaper letters: "This is /m/." (not the letter name, but the sound)
- Trace it slowly with two fingers while making the sound. Invite the child to try.

Period Two: Recognition—"Can you show me. . .?"

- Lay out 2–3 known letters or items.
- Ask: "Can you show me /m/?"
- Mix the order and repeat. This is an interactive step—meant for practice, not testing.

Period Three: Recall—"What is this?"

- Point to one letter and ask, "What sound is this?"
- If the child hesitates or gives an incorrect answer, return to Period One calmly and without pressure.

This method works best when used consistently over time. It strengthens your ability to guide Montessori lessons with intention and reinforces the Montessori principle of guiding without pressuring.

Practice Before You Present

Montessori guides don't wing it. They practice. You should too.

Before giving a lesson:

- Handle the materials yourself
- Move slowly and intentionally
- Mentally walk through each step
- Eliminate unnecessary words
- Decide where you'll sit, how you'll invite your child, and how the activity will end

This practice gives you the clarity your child needs in your lesson presentations.

> ### *How to Deliver a Montessori Lesson: Step-by-Step*
>
> Montessori lessons are demonstrations, not explanations. Your child learns by watching and doing—not by being told what to do.
>
> 1. **Prepare Yourself:** Practice until the steps feel calm and clear.
> 2. **Prepare the Environment:** Everything should be in place before the lesson begins. No searching for a missing pitcher mid-demonstration.
> 3. **Invite the Child:** "Would you like to see something new?" An invitation, not a command.
> 4. **Sit Beside Them:** Sit on your child's dominant side so they can mirror your movements with ease.
> 5. **Demonstrate Silently:** Let your hands do the teaching. Speak only if needed—and only after you've modeled.
> 6. **Offer the Work:** Pause. Then say, "Would you like to try?" Let them take over.
> 7. **Step Back and Observe:** Don't correct. Don't interfere. Just watch. Let them experience it for themselves.
> 8. **Re-Present Only When Necessary:** If they ask or seem stuck, say, "Would you like to see it again?"
> 9. **End While Interest Is High:** Avoid dragging it out. A short, successful experience is better than one that ends in frustration.
> 10. **Restore the Environment Together:** Model the full cycle of work—beginning, middle, and end.

Starting in Upper Elementary Tips (Ages 9–12)

Older children who are new to Montessori benefit from greater ownership of learning. Instead of demonstrating lessons in full, co-create the process. Ask open-ended questions like, "What materials do we need to wrap this box?" or "How would you set up a folding station?" Let them take the lead, reflect on the experience, and refine the process.

Introduce weekly planning meetings where they can identify goals, areas of interest, and essential work. Guide them to differentiate between "must-dos" and "may-dos," and support them in managing their time and responsibilities.

In upper elementary, collaboration and relevance are key. Invite them into household responsibilities, real-world problem-solving, and practical applications. For core subjects like math and language, consider working with a Montessori-aligned coach or consultant who can help with placement and determine whether a complementary curriculum is appropriate. The goal is to build autonomy, while anchoring learning in meaning and responsibility.

Lesson Planning as a Beginner

Keep it simple. Focus on:

- Grace and courtesy
- Practical life
- Maintaining shelves as outlined in Section 3
- Staying present for the duration of the work cycle and helping your child navigate the transition
- Writing down observations

Best Practices for the Beginner Montessorian

Use Instagram, Pinterest, and plug-and-play resources for inspiration—not as scripts or pacing guides. Avoid comparing what your child is doing to someone else's highlight reel. Start with a short list of "next possible lessons" based on what you observe. If your child is still engaged with a work, let them continue. Progress in Montessori is not measured by how fast you move, but by how deeply your child engages. Montessori is a practice of presence and patience.

You Are Not Just a Teacher

Remember, in your homeschool, you are:

- A guide
- A model
- An observer
- A co-learner

You are also a parent. Your relationship matters more than any presentation. Your calm presence, your willingness to adjust, and your respect for your child's pace are more important than getting the lesson "right."

Montessori homeschooling starts with a tone. A tone of respect. A tone of focus. A tone of calm engagement.

If your child walks away from their first lesson feeling trusted, interested, and capable—you've succeeded.

What Comes Next

The next chapter walks through exactly what to do on Day 1, Week 1, and Month 1. You learn how to choose lessons based on readiness, how to support your child without micromanaging, and how to build rhythm through repetition—not rush. This is where your homeschool becomes real—not perfect, but alive.

Let's take the next step.

Thoughts from the Frontlines

What it really looks like to give lessons at home—without performance pressure or perfectionism.

Tiffany: Bilingual homeschooling mother of three, navigating Montessori without an educational background

"The three-period lesson has become my go-to. Once I practiced it enough, it became second nature. My husband even uses it now with our three-year-old! In the beginning, I felt nervous about doing it perfectly, especially since I didn't have an educational background. But I've learned that staying calm and following their lead works better than trying to deliver a flawless lesson. If they're not ready, I let them put the material away. Then, later—after we've had time to regulate—we talk through what happened. That space helps everything go smoother the next time."

(continued)

(continued)

Viviana: Doctor of Nursing Practice turned business-owning homeschool mom

"My oldest was used to being told what to do in virtual school, so even when we started Montessori, she waited for direction. Over time, modeling lessons and giving her space to choose helped her gain confidence. I love how the three-period lesson creates both clarity and freedom. I've also found that calm background music signals focus time. It helps me stay grounded as I guide—not just teach—especially when my toddler and preschooler are in the room watching too."

Mae-Lin: Trauma-informed mom homeschooling one child

"I used to get so frustrated when I'd prep a beautiful lesson and my daughter wasn't interested or got distracted. But I realized I wasn't preparing myself. Now, I practice the lesson the night before and mentally rehearse what role I'll need to play: guide, peer, or parent. I try to model the work alongside her, especially for math and language—she learns best when I'm participating. And if she wants to explore a material before I present it? That's okay. I've learned to breathe, pause, and meet her where she is."

To learn more about the families featured throughout this book, you'll find their bios in the appendix.

17

What to Do on Day 1, Week 1, Month 1

A Step-by-Step Road Map

You're standing at the starting line—your first official day of Montessori homeschooling! Maybe the shelf is set up, the materials are neatly arranged, and the snacks are prepped. But you're still wondering:

"What exactly do I do now?"

This chapter is here to take out the guesswork. You don't need to be perfect. But you do need to be prepared. Let's walk through exactly what to do during your first day, your first week, and your first month—so you can start with confidence and clarity.

> **NOTE** The examples in this chapter are geared toward children ages 3–9 who are new to Montessori. If you are beginning with an older child, see the Upper Elementary Adaptation Tip at the end of the chapter for specific guidance.

Before you dive into the practical steps, reframe your expectations. Remember these important points about being a Montessori guide:

- You are not re-creating school at home.
- Your goal is not to "teach lessons" on Day 1.
- You are building trust, rhythm, and independence—from the ground up.

Your role is to orient, observe, and guide. And that begins long before academics.

Day 1: Orientation, Grace and Courtesy, and Expectations

Step 1: Orient Your Child to the Space

Just like a new employee needs an office tour, your child needs an introduction to their new learning environment.

Walk them through:

- What this space is for ("This is a place where you can work and learn.")
- What each shelf holds ("This is the language shelf with your reading, writing, and handwriting work. These are the readers. This is the Moveable Alphabet, etc. This is the math shelf with your operations and facts work. This is the stamp game. These are the Golden Beads, and so on.")
- Where supplies belong and how to return them
  Model everything slowly. Let them practice. Keep it simple and concrete.

Step 2: Introduce Grace and Courtesy

As we discussed in Chapter 16, grace and courtesy lessons are not add-ons—they're essential. On Day 1, begin with just a few simple, meaningful lessons to set the tone:

- What's off-limits during work time (toys, TV, noisy games)
- How to interrupt politely (hand on shoulder, wait quietly)
- How to carry a tray with two hands
- How to walk around someone's rug

These lessons show your child how to exist in this new environment with care and respect. They introduce expectations through demonstration and practice—not rules and correction.

Treat these the way you would any academic lesson: present them clearly, model the behavior, and invite your child to try. Use a three-period lesson where applicable and continue reinforcing them throughout your day. These are soft skills that support concentration, autonomy, and peace.

Step 3: Ground the Work in Process, Not Product

Rather than diving into academics or introducing complex new materials, begin with practical life and familiar shelf activities. These were introduced in Section 3 and are ideal for the first few days because they give you the opportunity to reinforce expectations and rhythm without overwhelming your child.

This work:

- Provides high-interest, accessible experiences
- Reinforces order, concentration, and independence
- Allows your child to succeed early and build confidence
- Gives you space to observe and support your child's behavior gently
- Offers opportunities to reinforce grace and courtesy in real time

Your role here is not to focus on outcomes but to teach process: how to choose work, how to engage with it, and how to restore it. These foundational routines will anchor everything else.

Sample Day 1 Work Period Flow (Three-Hour Cycle)

- **Begin with Connection:** A short read-aloud, a calendar activity, and/or a song to signal the start of work time and build shared focus.
- **Present 1–2 Practical Life Lessons:** Choose high-interest activities such as folding, sweeping, or snack preparation—something purposeful and accessible.
- **Snack Time Outdoors:** Invite your child to prepare a snack (e.g., slicing fruit, pouring water) and enjoy it outside. This honors their movement and need for transition.
- **Return to Indoor Work:** Offer a transition shelf activity—such as matching, sorting, or a puzzle—to help ease back into focus.

- **Parallel Work:** Sit nearby and engage in your own quiet task (reading, journaling, planning) while your child continues working independently.
- **Observation Opportunity:** As your child works, make notes. Resist the urge to correct. Simply watch, and begin to notice patterns of interest or challenge.

Let Day 1 be about *how*—not *what*.

Week 1: Observation and the Work Cycle

Step 1: Observe Without Intervening

Set aside at least 30 minutes each day to watch your child work. Choose a quiet task for yourself—journaling, reading, or one of your child's shelf works—so you don't hover. Watch for:

- What draws their attention?
- Where do they seem to struggle?
- What do they repeat?

Take notes. This is the foundation of your planning.

Step 2: Introduce the Cycle of Work

The Montessori cycle of work includes:

1. Choosing a workspace
2. Choosing work from the shelf
3. Engaging in the work
4. Restoring the work when finished

At first, model the whole cycle. Narrate your steps. Invite your child to try. Repeat this process multiple times, each day during the week, with different works.

Step 3: Prioritize Consistency and Focus

This isn't the week to debut the Stamp Game or grammar boxes. Instead, focus on showing up consistently, creating a predictable flow to your cycle, staying present, and engaging in work that promotes concentration and independence from the Practical Life and Transition shelves. If you'd like, begin to layer in books, stories, or one unit study topic that align with your child's interests and spark curiosity.

The goal is not coverage—it's to anchor the rhythm and deepen focus.

Month 1: Rhythm, Refinement, and Trusting the Process

Step 1: Strengthen the Daily Rhythm Through Practice

You laid the foundation for a daily rhythm in Chapter 15—now it's time to bring that rhythm to life. This first month is not about finding the perfect schedule; it's about helping your child recognize the natural flow of the day.

Consistency is key. Focus on repeating the same general structure each day, especially the work cycle. The more familiar and dependable the rhythm becomes, the more trust and independence your child will build.

Keep it flexible, but consistent enough that your child begins to anticipate what comes next.

Step 2: Refine, Don't Overhaul

Observe and adjust your environment slowly and intentionally. Focusing specifically on the shelf:

Ask yourself:

- Are they choosing the same works?
- Are they completing the cycle of work?
- Are they growing in independence?

Make small changes based on what you literally observe—not what you assume.

A few examples of simple changes that won't throw off your flow but may motivate engagement:

- Change dry-pouring lentils to chickpeas for novelty
- Swap a tray for a basket or a wooden cardholder to freshen the display
- Elevate cards on a stand instead of placing them flat on the tray

Think of your shelf like a storefront window—your job is to curate, not clutter. You can't be consistent without actually being consistent. So before you switch something out, ask: *Have I really given this enough time and opportunity?* It's not always the child or the work that's the problem—it might be your implementation, presentation, or display.

Step 3: Shift from Teacher to Guide

Month 1 is when you are stepping fully into your role:

- Prepare the environment
- Observe before presenting
- Step back and allow ownership

This is the rhythm of Montessori: prepare, present, observe, refine.

Tips for getting started with confidence:

- **Don't overplan.** Simplicity is your friend.
- **Keep a notebook.** Document progress, questions, and observations.
- **Be consistent.** Rhythm beats novelty every time.
- **Model focus.** Do your own work alongside your child.
- **Go slow.** This isn't a sprint. It's a foundation.

Upper Elementary Adaptation Tip (Ages 9–12)

If your child is 9 or older and new to Montessori, your focus as an adult remains the same Day 1, Week 1, Month 1. Orientation is still necessary, as is establishing a rhythm, and maintaining a consistent and prepared environment. Given your child's stage of development, you may consider some adaptations to invite collaboration, like:

- Touring the space together. Invite their input on organizing materials.
- Creating a shared rhythm and brainstorm expectations together.

- Assigning a work cycle responsibility. Let them choose tasks that maintain your learning space to own (e.g., watering plants, dusting the shelves).
- Starting with real-life learning instead of a read aloud. Include journaling, nature study, or independent reading.
- Exploring a passion-drive, research-based project instead of a thematic unit.
- Using weekly check-ins to co-create a plan for core subjects, focusing on both interests and skill development.

At this stage, engagement is rooted in relevance. The child must see purpose in the work. Let them help shape it.

For core academics like math and writing, work with a coach or consultant to determine the best entry point. A supplemental curriculum may be needed at first, but aim to integrate it into the Montessori mindset over time.

What Comes Next

The next chapter looks at common roadblocks that come up during your first month—and how to move through them with clarity and calm.

For now, return to this road map as often as needed. Let it anchor your steps when you feel unsure. You don't need to be perfect. You just need the next step.

Now you have one.

Thoughts from the Frontlines

Your first steps—calm, intentional, and connection-focused—not curriculum-driven.

Sarah: Homesteading mom of four, juggling ages 2–9 in a Montessori homeschool

"We didn't start with academics. On day one, we walked into the space and talked about how to care for it. I introduced grace and

(continued)

(continued)

courtesy lessons—how to roll out a mat, how to ask for help, how to return materials. That first week, I focused entirely on observation. I noticed what materials they gravitated toward and where the environment wasn't working. One of my biggest wins that month was realizing I had to group certain lessons—like geometry or science—so I wasn't stretched too thin. But I never would've seen that if I hadn't paused and watched first."

Wennie: Nurse and mom of two, Montessori homeschooling in a small apartment

"Our first week wasn't picture-perfect, but we started with a rhythm. I played soft music and introduced just a few works. I explained to my kids what to do when I was working with the other sibling. I didn't expect full independence right away. Instead, I focused on one success: getting through a short work cycle with calm. I've learned that starting small, especially with two kids under five, is not just okay—it's essential. It gave me the confidence to keep going."

Wilka: Bilingual, working mom of one, rethinking homeschool as a mindset

"When we started over with Montessori, I had to unlearn the checklist approach I used in our first year. Day one wasn't about lessons. It was about sitting with my daughter and noticing what made her curious. I kept the shelves light and introduced just the calendar and a couple of works I knew she'd enjoy. During that first month, I started setting up our reset routine—a soft alarm that lets us both know when it's time to wrap up and tidy. It's those small rituals that have helped build our rhythm more than any curriculum plan ever could."

To learn more about the families featured throughout this book, you'll find their bios in the appendix.

18

Common Roadblocks

The Early Challenges That Shape You as a Guide

No matter how well you've prepared, the early stages of Montessori homeschooling come with challenges. Some days will feel seamless, while others may leave you questioning everything. This is completely normal. The transition from conventional education—or even no structured education at all—to Montessori education at home is a *process, not a single event.*

Starting your Montessori homeschool journey is exciting—but like any new beginning, it will test your assumptions, your habits, and your patience. And that's not a sign you're doing it wrong. That's exactly what transformation looks like.

This chapter walks through the most common stumbling blocks new Montessori homeschoolers face, not just to validate your experience, but to help you reflect honestly, respond with purpose, and stay focused on what truly matters: growing as a guide and creating an environment where your child can flourish.

Grappling with Your Own Expectations

Let's be honest. You've spent weeks preparing. You've read the philosophy. You've arranged the shelves. So when your child seems uninterested, distracted, or even resistant, it's easy to think:

- What am I doing wrong?
- Is this working?
- Why won't they engage with the materials I carefully set out?

Here's what's usually happening: you're still shifting from a traditional schooling mindset into a Montessori one.

But this isn't about lowering your expectations—it's about understanding how those expectations are met.

In Montessori, we hold high expectations. We expect children to develop independence, self-regulation, and a sense of responsibility. But we also understand that these qualities aren't outcomes we demand—they're outcomes we prepare for.

It's not about whether or not you expect your child to make their bed in the morning. You do—from toddlerhood. But how you expect it to happen evolves with development. A toddler might place the pillows while you guide the sheets. A six-year-old might complete the task with support. A 10-year-old might take full ownership. The expectation is consistent. The path to mastery is not.

Frustration tends to arise when we expect performance without preparing for the process. We assume that because we said it, the child should do it. But in Montessori, we educate to potential, not just current performance. We provide opportunity. We make space for practice.

So instead of asking:

- Did we finish everything today?

Ask:

- Did my child practice something meaningful?
- Did I give them an opportunity to try?
- Did I model what I hope to see?

Story: *Sarah was frustrated that her five-year-old refused to touch the sandpaper letters she had lovingly purchased. But after observing him for a few days, she noticed he was deeply engaged in practical life—pouring, scrubbing, sweeping. That's where his developmental need was. Two weeks later, he picked up the moveable alphabet and started spelling on his own.*

The lesson? It's not about the lesson you're ready to teach—it's about the learning they're ready to absorb. Expectations are not the problem. But performance-based thinking is. Let go of how you think it "should" look—and lean into what's truly unfolding.

In Montessori, we guide with clarity and hold space for growth. The work will come—in its time.

Letting Go of Control

One of the first—and most confronting—shifts in Montessori homeschooling is the need to let go of control. Not just over the schedule or the outcomes, but over how learning unfolds.

You want it to go well. You want your child to engage. You want to feel like it's working. But in Montessori, we understand that the child is not within our control—we can only control ourselves and our environment. Learning to channel our need for control appropriately is hard. The adult doesn't manage learning—they guide it. That means allowing space for discovery and resisting the urge to intervene or correct when things don't go as expected.

Letting go of control is difficult because it asks us to trust something we can't always see right away: internal development. We've been conditioned to believe that if we just set everything up "right," our child will take off independently. And when that doesn't happen, frustration creeps in—not because we expected too much, but because we didn't understand how much time, practice, and presence would be required to reach that expectation.

We do expect children to become independent, responsible, and respectful because we know them to be capable. But we recognize that those traits develop through consistent, scaffolded experience, not instant compliance. No one wakes up at 16 suddenly able to manage responsibility. That capacity is built through repetition, support, and opportunities for practice provided within the environments we grow up in over time.

Control belongs to the child.

In moments that feel frustrating or unclear, ask yourself:

- Have I modeled this skill consistently?
- Have I taught this skill explicitly?
- Have I allowed enough time for practice?
- Am I holding on to control where I could instead offer trust?

Montessori isn't a system of rewards, punishments, or pressure. It's a method build on trust, clarity, and observation. When in doubt: take a deep breath and get curious. Growth is already happening.

Managing Resistance or Disinterest

Every Montessori homeschooler will face days—or even weeks—when their child resists the work or seems disinterested entirely. This isn't failure. It's feedback. And often, it's not about the materials at all.

Children transitioning into a Montessori homeschool environment may be navigating a number of internal shifts:

- **They may associate learning with pressure or performance.** If they've come from a traditional school, they may expect to be corrected or tested.
- **They may be unsure of what's expected.** Montessori doesn't look like the structure they're used to—and that unfamiliarity can feel unsettling.
- **They may lack the internal rhythm for sustained focus.** Self-direction takes practice. The ability to engage independently doesn't appear overnight.
- **They may still be assessing the power dynamic.** "Is this real? Can I really choose? Are you going to make me?" They're looking for consistency—and clarity.

In these moments, your role is to pause and observe. Ask yourself:

- Are the choices too open-ended or overwhelming?
- Has your child had enough movement before being asked to concentrate?

- Are they avoiding work that's too difficult because they lack the prerequisite skills?

These aren't excuses. They're insights. And they help you respond rather than react.

Revisiting Grace and Courtesy

If your child isn't completing the cycle of work—choosing, engaging, restoring—go back and model it again. Grace and courtesy isn't a one-and-done concept. It's the structure through which we teach expectations.

Use clear, simple language:

> "I'm going to roll up my rug and return my work now."

Repetition builds fluency. Don't assume that because they've seen it once, it's been internalized.

Offering Choices Within Limits

Avoid asking, "Do you want to do school?" That's not a real question—it's a setup for resistance.

Instead, offer two real, purposeful options:

> "Would you like to do pouring or color tablets first?"

Montessori freedom is always paired with responsibility. When a child is resisting, they may be seeking clarity more than control. Clear, limited choices help rebuild a sense of agency while still honoring the prepared environment.

> **REMEMBER** Resistance is not a signal to abandon the method—it's a call to deepen your practice of it. Stay consistent. Observe with curiosity. Model what matters.

You don't need to push. You need to anchor.

Transitioning from Traditional School? Expect a Detox Period

If your child is coming out of a traditional school setting, you're not just shifting environments—you're shifting mindsets. That kind of change takes time. During this time, your child may:

- Resist structured work
- Push boundaries
- Seem unmotivated, bored, or disengaged
- Ask, "Why aren't we doing real school?"

This is normal. They're unlearning habits of compliance, external validation, performance-based thinking, and habits of passive learning. They're recalibrating their nervous system. You're recalibrating too.

> "A good rule of thumb is to expect one month of deschooling for every year they spent in school."

You might wonder if you made the wrong choice. You might panic when your child doesn't "want to do anything." That's not a red flag—it's a rite of passage.

Hold steady. Keep your rhythm. Keep showing up with calm, clear expectations and trust the method to do its work. The detox may be messy, but it's making room for something deeper.

Blaming the Child Instead of the Setup

When something isn't working, our instinct is often to correct the child. But in Montessori, we focus on the environment.

Many early struggles—disinterest, distraction, lack of follow-through—aren't behavioral problems. They're environmental ones. Shelves might be overstimulating. Materials might be too difficult. Transitions might be rushed. Interruptions might be constant.

Before you correct the child, pause and ask:

- Is this environment calm, orderly, and beautiful?
- Are the shelves uncluttered?
- Are the works prepared and developmentally aligned?

Sometimes, small adjustments can restore engagement without adding more lessons or pressure:

- Swap lentils for chickpeas in scooping work.
- Display matching cards upright in a business card holder.
- Trade a wooden tray for a woven basket to change the sensory appeal.

In Montessori, the environment is the child's teacher. The environment is social, emotional, and physical. You are part of the environment. Keep refining it.

Thoughts from the Frontlines

When it feels like it's not working—pause, observe, adjust. This is part of the process.

Mae-Lin: Veteran, perfectionist, and mother healing through Montessori

"One of my biggest roadblocks was thinking my daughter would be self-directed right away. I thought, 'I've prepared the environment, now she'll just take off'. But without peers around like in a classroom, she needed me to model, to co-work. Once I embraced that 80% of her work would be collaborative in these early years, everything shifted. I stopped expecting her to just know what to do—and I stopped taking her struggle personally. The frustration was information, not failure."

Fatema: SAHM of two in Saudi Arabia, navigating commitment fears

"I used to think I couldn't be consistent enough to do Montessori 'right'. That fear kept me in a cycle of starting and stopping. What helped me break that was creating systems to support *me*. I realized I was the biggest variable. I had to prepare myself, not just the shelves. Now I check in with myself weekly, reflect on what's working or not, and remind myself: this is a long game, and I don't have to be perfect to be effective."

(continued)

(continued)

Tiffany: Colombian–American mom of three, working toward biliteracy

"Planning nearly broke me. I kept asking, 'What if I miss something important?' But then I realized I was treating Montessori like traditional school—thinking in grades and checklists. Once I understood that she had three years in this plane, and that repetition and observation were the real roadmap, I stopped rushing. I remind myself: just because she doesn't master something right away doesn't mean I'm behind. It means we're learning."

To learn more about the families featured throughout this book, you'll find their bios in the appendix.

19

Supporting the Whole Child

Socialization, Emotional Growth, and Your Role as the Anchor

Your shelves are prepared. Your lessons are taking shape. You're easing into rhythm. But beneath all of this—the structure, the method, the materials—lies something deeper and more enduring: your child's emotional life and their need to belong.

Montessori homeschooling is about *whole* child development. That means honoring the emotional, social, spiritual, and relational dimensions of your child's experience—not just their academic growth.

This chapter is here to help you do that—not by giving you a checklist of "socialization activities," but by exploring how Montessori supports social-emotional growth and how you, the adult, are one of its most powerful catalysts.

The Myth of the "Unsocialized Homeschooler"

If you've been homeschooling for more than five minutes, someone has probably asked, "But what about socialization?" It's a common concern, but it stems from a misunderstanding. Socialization isn't about being surrounded by 25 same-age peers all day. It's about learning how to communicate, collaborate, and participate meaningfully in a community.

Montessori approaches this through:

- **Grace and courtesy lessons** that model social behavior explicitly
- **Mixed-age interaction** that promotes empathy and leadership
- **Real-world experiences** that foster genuine connection and contribution

Socialization in a Montessori homeschool happens organically—through work, play, conversation, and shared living. But it does require intention. You are not replicating the social environment of school. You are creating one that supports your values and your child's needs.

You Are the Anchor

You are not just your child's emotional reference point—you are also the builder of their first community. Whether you're new to homeschooling or years in, your consistency and initiative shape the social and emotional life of your home.

Belonging doesn't happen by chance—it's cultivated. When you introduce yourself to neighbors, plan a casual meetup, or simply make yourself visible in your local spaces, you're modeling what it means to participate in a community. You're teaching your child that relationships are built, not assigned.

You don't have to be socially outgoing or endlessly available. You just have to be willing to take the first step. That's what it means to be the anchor.

Building an Intentional Social Rhythm

One of the greatest challenges in modern homeschooling is isolation—not just for children, but also for adults. We've lost the village. Many of us are parenting in physical or emotional silos, with no default community to lean on. Community *must* be cultivated. It won't fall into your lap.

This section discusses how to start building a community—not just for your child, but for you too.

Start with Your Own Street

- **Meet your neighbors:** Yes, knock on a door. Start with "Hi, I'm new to homeschooling and trying to meet more families around here." It's brave—but brave builds bridges.
- **Be seen outside:** Play in the front yard. Take walks. Say hello. Being visible invites connection.
- **Make a flyer:** Create a neighborhood kid meetup or nature walk. Post it in your local library or online neighborhood forum.

Design a Weekly Social Rhythm

A strong social rhythm is predictable but flexible and does not interfere with your work cycles. For example:

- Monday: Nature group
- Wednesday: Co-op or library class
- Friday: Park day with neighbors or homeschool friends

Start with one social anchor per week and build from there.

Facilitate Mixed-Age Experiences

Mixed-age interaction is one of Montessori's most underrated gifts. Try:

- Inviting siblings to work together on a task
- Hosting a backyard "project day" with kids of different ages
- Asking your child to help a younger child with snack prep or practical life work

These interactions build empathy, leadership, and adaptability.

Create Organic Play Opportunities

Unstructured play isn't optional—it's essential. Carve out regular windows for:

- Fort building
- Imaginative play
- Free outdoor time

If your child doesn't have ready access to peers, consider creating a rotating backyard playdate group with a few like-minded families.

What About **Your** *Social Connections?*

Let's not pretend: homeschooling can be lonely. And many of us—especially those raised in traditional school systems—don't have the social-emotional toolkit to build adult friendships easily.

But connection is vital. You can't pour from an empty cup.

- Join a homeschool group for parents, even if it's virtual.
- Invite another parent for a walk-and-talk while the kids play.
- Start a monthly book club or family dinner potluck—it doesn't have to be fancy.
- Say yes to low-stakes invites, even if you're tired. Sometimes the effort opens the door to something real.

You are not just creating a learning life for your child. You're creating a *life*. Don't forget to include yourself in that.

The Nervous System Comes First

Montessori environments are designed to be peaceful for a reason. A dys-regulated nervous system can't absorb new information. Calm is not just aesthetic. It's a requirement for learning.

What this might look like:

- Use low lighting, soft music, or quiet rituals
- Offer breaks without punishment
- Invite—not insist
- Observe with curiosity, not control
- Checking in with yourself and taking five minutes to meditate before the start of each work cycle

When a child feels safe, they are more available for learning, relationship, and growth.

A Whole Child Perspective

Academic success is not the goal of Montessori homeschooling. Wholeness is. You're building a home that teaches your child:

- How to relate to others
- How to communicate with respect
- How to manage their emotions
- How to contribute to their world
- How to find belonging

Those things won't come from a workbook. They'll come from you. Your modeling. Your relationships. Your intentionality.

Supporting the whole child isn't a subject. It's not a lesson plan. It's a way of living and relating. You are not just raising a student. You're raising a person. A friend. A future collaborator. A future parent. A citizen of the world.

So yes, teach them math. Teach them to read. But just as importantly:

- Teach them to listen.
- Teach them to repair.
- Teach them to breathe and begin again.

You can't do this perfectly. But you *can* do it consciously. Don't underestimate the power of what feels ordinary. As their parent, you are offering something deeper than curriculum. You are helping them become themselves.

Thoughts from the Frontlines

Real education isn't just what happens on the shelf—it's how we show up for our children as whole people. Montessori doesn't separate academics from life; it honors the child as a social, emotional, and spiritual being.

Sarah: Homesteading mother of four, raising a family on purpose
"I used to think socialization meant signing my kids up for every group I could find. But what I've seen is that the most powerful

(continued)

(continued)

emotional development happens right here at home—when they're learning to live alongside each other, take responsibility for our animals, solve conflicts without adult interference, and contribute meaningfully. That's what builds character. When I do observe something that needs support—like a breakdown in communication—I bring it up with my husband, and we address it as a team. Montessori helps me see those moments not as interruptions to learning, but as the learning."

Viviana: Doctor-turned-homeschool mom of three daughters
"We had to unlearn the idea that kids need to be told everything in order to learn. Once we started following our daughters' emotional cues and creating consistency—not just in the schedule, but in how we responded to their needs—everything changed. Our three-year-old used to resist everything. Now, because she knows what's coming next and feels seen, she participates joyfully. That kind of emotional regulation wasn't taught to me growing up, but we're learning it together now."

Destiny: Single mother focused on global Black identity and emotional liberation
"For us, supporting the whole child means prioritizing belonging. Not just belonging in a peer group, but in their own body, their culture, their voice. My son is part of a global story, and our learning reflects that. When I think about his social-emotional development, it's less about making sure he's around enough other kids, and more about: Does he feel safe to express hard feelings? Does he feel agency in his choices? Is he growing in compassion? That's the work. Montessori gives us the tools—but it's the connection that makes them come alive."

To learn more about the families featured throughout this book, you'll find their bios in the appendix.

20

Observation and Repetition

Learning to See and Support Growth

If Montessori education had a secret superpower, it would be observation. Not the casual kind where you glance at your child while scrolling your phone—but deliberate, structured, purposeful observation. This is not passive watching. It's an intentional practice rooted in curiosity and deep respect.

Observation is the heart of Montessori. It informs how you guide, how you prepare the environment, and how you respond to the unique needs of your child. Observation isn't a bonus—it's foundational.

But observation on its own isn't enough. What you notice must shape how you respond. That's where repetition comes in.

If observation and assessment had a child, it would be repetition. Repetition is how children internalize, master, and revisit learning. It's how they build independence and confidence. And for you, it's how you gather insight—not through quizzes and checklists, but through presence and pattern-seeking.

Let's talk about how these two practices—observation and repetition—work together and how to use them to measure what matters most in your Montessori homeschool.

Observation: The First Step to Understanding

The goal of Montessori is to observe, not to judge, but to understand. You're not scanning for errors or rushing to correct. You're watching with stillness and curiosity. Observe to see what your child is showing you—not what you expect to see.

When you observe the Montessori way, you:

- Slow down.
- Step back.
- Watch without interference.
- Listen with your eyes as much as your ears.
- Take in the whole child—their body language, pace, choices, and emotional tone.

Think of it like being a scientist in your own home. You aren't jumping to conclusions; you're gathering data. Instead of asking, "What lesson should I give next?" try asking, "What is my child telling me with their actions?"

"This simple shift—from teaching to seeing—changes everything. It turns homeschooling from performance-based teaching into responsive, growth-centered learning."

Observation also becomes your most reliable way of tracking progress. Not with formal tests, but with repeated patterns of engagement: the way a child returns to a material, how long they concentrate, what challenges them, and what they are drawn to next. It's subtle, yes. But it's powerful.

Repetition: The Child's Path to Mastery

Here's what many new homeschoolers miss: learning doesn't happen at the moment of presentation—it happens after. Through practice. Through trying, failing, adjusting, and trying again.

Repetition is not about drilling facts or forcing practice. It's the child's *intrinsic* method of making sense of the world. They repeat not because we tell them to—but because they are working toward mastery. Repetition is how they strengthen neural connections, refine motor skills, and deepen understanding.

In Montessori, you don't rush this process. You protect it. You normalize it. You build an environment that welcomes it.

Think of any skill you've mastered—cooking, writing, learning a language, playing an instrument. Did it happen after one lesson? Of course not. You practiced. You returned. You got curious about your mistakes and proud of your progress. Children are no different.

This process of repetition isn't just academic. It supports:

- Memory and long-term retention.
- Executive functioning and planning.
- Emotional regulation through predictable routines.
- Confidence and perseverance through self-directed effort.

Sometimes repetition looks identical—doing the same puzzle or pouring work again and again. Other times, it evolves. The child adds a twist, uses new materials, or works in a new location. Either way, the repetition is meaningful.

How Observation and Repetition Work Together

Observation helps you know *what* to repeat and *when* to move forward. It reveals where the child is in their learning journey—what's still being processed and what's becoming fluent.

Instead of asking, "Did they complete the task?" ask:

- Are they returning to this material?
- Are they more focused today than yesterday?
- Are they showing signs of fluency, or are they still exploring?
- Are they joyful, curious, or frustrated?

Your role isn't to rush in and fix. It's to notice. When you observe regularly, you'll know when to:

- Re-present a lesson for clarity.
- Offer a variation or extension to renew interest.
- Step back and let the child repeat without interruption.

This is what authentic Montessori assessment looks like. It's quiet. Ongoing. Responsive. Grounded in trust.

Getting Started with Observation

You don't need a complex system or software. You need a chair, a pen, and a few intentional minutes. Start small:

- Choose a consistent time—maybe during your child's independent work cycle or free play.
- Sit in a neutral spot where you can watch unobtrusively.
- Keep a simple two-column notebook or digital note.

Use this structure:

Noticing (What You See, Literally)	Thought-Catcher (Judgements, Assessments)
"He chose the spindle box"	"Is he mastering quantity to symbol recognition?"
"She got frustrated during pouring"	"That pitcher is too heavy"

Resist the urge to overanalyze in the moment. Most of your energy should go toward collecting data—observing patterns and habits. Let interpretation happen later, during your planning and reflection time.

The Role of Extensions and Variations

In Montessori, repetition isn't limited to exact repetition of a lesson or material over and over. Repetition is *any* form of work that allows the child to revisit or practice the same skill or concept. This includes variations on the original activity, learning extensions, themed adaptations, observing another child, and even tutoring a peer or sibling.

One of the greatest privileges of homeschooling is the ability to observe repetition throughout the day—both inside and outside the prepared learning space. In Montessori homeschooling, **variations and extensions become especially important** because our physical environment carries more responsibility in the absence of peer modeling and classroom dynamics.

As the child gains fluency, their interest may begin to wane—not because the work no longer matters, but because their mind is seeking a new layer of challenge. This is where Montessori's intentional use of *extensions* and *variations* becomes powerful. They allow us to re-engage the child meaningfully with familiar material, offering fresh invitations for depth, creativity, and continued mastery.

- *Extensions* involve combining two or more known tasks or concepts in a way that builds on the child's previous work. For example:
  - After mastering spooning and color matching separately, the child might spoon red, blue, and yellow beads into color-coded bowls.
  - A child familiar with number rods and sandpaper numbers may be invited to pair the two in a matching game.
  - Once a child has practiced sound object boxes and metal insets, they might label drawn shapes with the corresponding beginning sounds.
- *Variations* involve changing a single element of a known activity to renew focus and deepen engagement:
  - Using dried lentils instead of beans in a pouring work.
  - Swapping out clear water for colored water or using a ladle instead of a spoon.
  - Offering a new tray, a different sponge, or smaller tongs.
  - Doing a familiar puzzle blindfolded or with a timer, adding an extra sensory or executive function challenge.

These small changes offer just the right amount of novelty—enough to spark interest without overwhelming the child's developing sense of order or fluency. But it's important to wait for the right moment. If your child is still choosing a material, that means it still serves a purpose. What may *look* like boredom to you could actually be a signal that they are moving into deeper concentration.

Sometimes, repetition is invisible. A child may trace the same sandpaper letter five days in a row—but each day, their strokes become more precise, their hand steadier, their mind more confident. Another child might return to a simple pouring work after several weeks, not because they forgot how, but because they're refining their control, now at a different developmental stage. You won't always see what's changing—but something always is.

From Seeds to Sustained Growth

Observation and repetition are the root system of Montessori. They're not flashy. They're not fast. But they're deep, steady, and reliable.

You won't always see the fruit right away. But under the surface, your child is building:

- A sense of trust in their own pace.
- A foundation of competence and confidence.
- A habit of deep engagement and inner motivation.

This is the long game. Stay present. Watch with wonder. Observe without judgment. Let repetition unfold as it's meant to. Because in Montessori, repetition isn't going backward. It's growing deeper roots.

Thoughts from the Frontlines

In Montessori, assessment doesn't come from tests—it comes from what we see, again and again. Repetition is not rote; it's the child's way of mastering a skill, deepening understanding, and building confidence. This chapter invites parents to become intentional noticers and to honor repetition as practice, not performance.

Wilka: Bicultural mother balancing part-time work and homeschool

"I set aside a dedicated observation time during our work cycle, but I also jot down spontaneous observations throughout the day. Sometimes I see my daughter revisiting an activity she hasn't touched in weeks, and I realize she's working through something—on her own timeline. That's what shifted for me this year: understanding that repetition isn't a sign of being stuck. It's a sign that she's finding her rhythm. Now, when I see her doing the same work again and again, I don't interrupt—I trust it."

Julianne: Minimalist mother in Northern Ireland, creating space for self-mastery

"At first, I thought observation meant just sitting with a notebook. But through Lynda's coaching, I began to see that observation of the child also meant observation of myself—of my reactions, my expectations. I started to notice when I wanted to correct too quickly, or when I was projecting my own impatience. That awareness helped me step back and really let my daughter repeat at her pace. I've learned that silence and space are powerful tools. Repetition is the child's teacher. I just needed to get out of the way."

Wennie: Nurse and mom of two, juggling work, toddlers, and Montessori

"It's easy to rush when you're short on time. But what I've seen is that when I give my kids time to return to the same material—especially after an imperfect session—they don't just complete it, they *own* it. I've had to remind myself: mastery isn't a performance. It's quiet. It looks like pouring water again, folding clothes again, asking the same question again. Observation helps me step out of 'teaching' mode and into guide mode. Repetition, I've realized, is where the real teaching happens—but it's not mine. It's theirs."

To learn more about the families featured throughout this book, you'll find their bios in the appendix.

5

Guiding the Montessori Learning Experience

Staying Grounded, Growing Forward

By now, you've done what many never dare to do: you've begun. You've reshaped your home, redefined your role, and introduced Montessori not just as a method—but as a way of life.

But here's the truth no one tells you upfront:

The hardest part of Montessori homeschooling isn't starting. It's *continuing*—with clarity, consistency, and confidence—after the novelty wears off.

This section is about what comes next: the slow, steady, often invisible work of deepening your practice.

It's about what you do when the shelves are no longer new, when your rhythm is tested, when comparison creeps in, and when you begin to wonder if you're "doing enough." It's in these moments that many homeschoolers start reaching outward—for curriculum, structure, validation. But what Montessori asks is that you go deeper *inward*—toward observation, trust, and alignment.

This section guides you through how to:

- **Adapt Montessori to your real, evolving family** without losing sight of the core principles.
- **Foster true independence** through practical strategies, consistent boundaries, and opportunities for responsibility.
- **Navigate discipline and conflict** using Montessori's approach to connection, not control.
- **Protect and nurture concentration** so your child can do the deep work of self-construction without constant redirection.

You'll also explore what it means to stay the course—not perfectly, but mindfully. This is the part of the journey where *integration* happens. Where theory becomes lifestyle. Where you become not just a parent who homeschools, but a prepared adult who leads a family culture of learning, respect, and growth.

This work is not easy. But it is meaningful. And it's worth it. Because the goal isn't just a successful homeschool year. It's a lifelong relationship with learning, with your child—and with yourself.

Let's keep going.

21

Adapting Montessori to Your Family

Making It Work Without Watering It Down

If you've made it this far, you've probably figured out that Montessori is not just a shelf aesthetic or a wholesome parenting trend. And if you're like most parents I work with, you're probably wondering something like: Okay, but how do I actually make this work for my real life? For my family? With our schedule, our budget, our kid who hates transitions, and me—an adult who's still figuring this all out too?

Let's talk about that.

Because yes—Montessori can work for you. But I need to clear something up right away: adapting Montessori doesn't mean distorting it until it's unrecognizable. It doesn't mean picking and choosing what's easiest or most convenient and tossing out the harder, slower parts that require your growth. It doesn't mean using the word "Montessori" while doing something entirely different and hoping for the same results.

Adapting Montessori means learning the method with integrity and applying it with intention. It means shaping your home and rhythm around your child's development—*not* the other way around. You don't need to do it perfectly. But you do need to understand *why* it works in order to apply it *in a way that does work*.

Montessori Is a Pedagogy, Not a Pinterest Trend

Let's pause on a word that doesn't often make it into casual homeschool conversations: pedagogy.

Pedagogy is the method and practice of teaching. It's not a vibe. It's not a list of hacks. And it's definitely not about replicating someone else's curated shelf display. Pedagogy means there is a *why* beneath the *what*—a structure, a logic, and a philosophy that informs every choice you make.

Montessori is a pedagogy because it gives you more than just what to present—it offers a road map for how to understand a child's development, how to respond to their needs, and how to build an environment that supports the full arc of human growth.

So when I talk about *adapting Montessori* to your family, I'm not talking about changing the method to suit your mood or aesthetic preferences. I'm talking about living the method in a way that is sustainable, authentic, and rooted in your family's reality—without compromising the method's integrity.

Montessori is flexible because it was designed to serve children across cultures, languages, neurotypes, and circumstances. That's what makes it powerful. But that flexibility comes with a responsibility: *to understand before you adapt.* You can only bend what you're willing to first learn the shape of.

What Adapting Doesn't Mean

Let's take a moment to clarify something that often gets misunderstood—especially in the homeschool worlds where we're juggling real-life constraints, mixed-age dynamics, and the daily realities of parenting.

Adapting Montessori doesn't mean diluting it. It doesn't mean casually borrowing form the method without understanding the system behind it. And it certainly doesn't mean skipping the structure and expecting the same results.

Here's what it *doesn't* look like:

- It doesn't mean sprinkling a few Montessori-inspired activities into your day and calling it "Montessori." This approach often leads to confusion—for the child and the adult—because it lacks the continuity that makes the method work.
- It doesn't mean renaming your chore chart "practical life" without carving out dedicated time for hands-on repetition, child ownership, and purposeful follow-through.
- It doesn't mean following your child's whims and labeling it "child-led" when what's happening is avoidance, disorganization, or overstimulation.
- It doesn't mean skipping the hard parts—like consistent routines, work cycle structure, or boundaries—because they feel inconvenient or uncomfortable.

Adaptation doesn't mean abandoning the integrity of the method. It doesn't mean cutting corners or simplifying Montessori into surface-level tasks and expecting deep developmental outcomes. It doesn't mean trading structure for spontaneity or skipping the prepared adult work because it feels like "less of a priority right now." And it certainly doesn't mean rebranding misalignment as "freedom" or "child-led." That's not fairness to the philosophy or to your child—it's frustration in disguise.

The truth is, Montessori *will* meet you where you are—but only if you're willing to meet it with humility, consistency, and a commitment to grow into your role as a guide. Not perfect—just prepared. And preparing.

What Adapting **Does** *Mean*

Adapting Montessori to your family means living the method—not mimicking it. It's not about perfect materials. It's about holding the *principles* of Montessori—even as the details flex to meet your family's unique rhythm, resources, and realities.

Here's what adapting *does* look like:

- Creating a learning rhythm that aligns with your household. Maybe that's a morning work cycle before you leave for your part-time job. Maybe it's afternoons after naps and errands. What matters is *consistency*— not conformity.

- Inviting your child into real life, not just shelf work. Folding laundry together can become a work of repetition for sorting, matching, or sequencing. Grocery shopping can become a spontaneous math or language experience. Montessori doesn't end at the shelf—it lives in the life you're already living.
- Choosing depth over breadth. Maybe this season, you focus on three core materials instead of 10. It's always better to do a few things well than to do "all the things" poorly. That's not falling behind—it's an act of trust. Mastery—yours and your child's—happens through repetition and connection, not volume.
- Accepting your limitations with honesty and adjusting with intention. Can't afford the moveable alphabet yet? Start with a simplified, high-quality version or offer targeted language work that builds the same foundational skills. Observe what your child is ready for before assuming you need more. Let readiness—not marketing—lead your decisions.

And yes—sometimes adapting means slowing down and tuning in. Resisting the urge to download more, plan more, buy more. It means protecting your energy and your child's focus. It means trusting that *you* are the prepared environment—and the most important material in your child's life.

REFLECTION PROMPT   Where in your home life can you make *space* for Montessori—not just on a shelf, but in your time, your energy, your conversations?

Individualized Doesn't Mean Personalized for the Adult

This is a big one—and often misunderstood or relabeled as "doing what's best for my family." Montessori is individualized, yes—but it's individualized for the *child*, not for the convenience, preferences, or learning style of the adult. That means the curriculum, environment, and pacing are all designed to meet the child where they are developmentally—not where we *wish* they were, and not where we *feel* most comfortable as the guide.

Here's what that might look like in practice:

- *You love reading*, but your child is more drawn to movement, puzzles, or sensorial challenges. So instead of filling the shelf with early readers and language cards, you lean into their interest in patterns, quantities, and hands-on exploration.

- *You might prefer a fast pace and daily variety*, but your child wants to do the same pouring work every single day for two weeks. Instead of rotating it out because *you're* bored, you slow down and observe: What skill are they refining? What's calling their attention? What might come next in this sequence? What variation can I offer?

TRY THIS   Ask yourself, *Am I planning this lesson because I think it's time. . . or because I've observed that my child is ready?* That one question can recenter your planning from adult-led to child-informed.

The Montessori adult learns to distinguish between child-led and adult-driven. When we confuse "individualized" for "personalized for the parent," we risk disrupting the very process we're trying to protect. Montessori honors the child's timeline. Our role is to prepare, observe, and respond—not to steer based on what feels easiest in the moment or impose our agenda on the child. This is where the work of *letting go* begins. And that means letting your child show you where they are, even if it's not where you expected them to be.

You Don't Need to Be Perfect—You Need to Be Prepared

Perfection is a myth that shows up loud and early in homeschooling. It whispers that if you just had the "right" shelf setup, the perfect routine, or the complete set of materials, then everything would fall into place. But that's not what Montessori asks of you.

Montessori doesn't need you to be flawless. It needs you to be observant, intentional, and prepared.

Prepared doesn't mean polished. It means present. It means you've thought ahead, set the environment with care, and are ready to respond to your child's real needs, not just react to their behavior. It means showing up each day not with all the answers, but with a posture of curiosity, trust, and a willingness to try again.

Preparation starts with you:

- You prepare your mindset: shifting from "What should I teach today?" to "What is my child ready for?"
- You prepare your space: keeping it simple, clean, and calm—not perfect, but purposeful.
- You prepare your role: recognizing that your job isn't to perform or entertain—it's to guide and step back when it's time.

Preparedness doesn't come from having all the materials or memorizing every lesson in the album. It comes from consistency, clarity, and presence. From knowing that you're here to walk *with* your child, not ahead of them.

You'll make mistakes. You'll miss cues. You'll prepare a lesson and realize it was too soon—or too late. That's part of the work. That's feedback. The prepared adult is not the perfect adult. The prepared adult keeps watching, keeps adjusting, and keeps coming back to the heart of the method: Follow the child.

REFLECTION PROMPT What part of your day could benefit from more preparation? What could you do the night before—or even five minutes before—that might help you show up more grounded?

Montessori Is a Lifelong Journey—Not a One-Time Setup

You don't "complete" Montessori. You live it. You grow into it. And as your understanding deepens, so does the method's impact.

There is no perfect rhythm, no one right shelf setup, no checklist that unlocks it all. But there *is* a path. And you're already on it. So yes—adapt the method. Just don't dilute it. Let it stretch you. Let it guide you. Let it change how you see your child—and yourself.

Because when you do, something beautiful happens. Montessori stops being something you "do." And starts becoming who you are becoming.

Thoughts from the Frontlines

This chapter reaffirms that Montessori is not a plug-and-play program—it's a living, evolving framework. Families are unique. Children are unique. And so your Montessori homeschool will be, too. Through real stories, we see how the method flexes around values, cultures, time, space, and seasons—while still staying grounded in core principles.

Tiffany: Colombian-American mother of three, navigating multilingual Montessori

"We don't have a perfect setup. Our homeschool room is in our master bedroom right now, and there are days I think, 'Is this Montessori enough?' But then I remind myself: it's not about looking like a classroom—it's about intention. We speak mostly Spanish at home, we're learning new languages, and I've had to adapt materials and presentations to reflect that. What matters is that the environment supports who my children are and how we live. That's authentic Montessori to me."

Mae-Lin: U.S. Army veteran, single child homeschooling, healing through the method

"There were so many times I got caught up in doing it 'right'. I wanted everything to align with the albums, the schedule, the phases. But life doesn't move that way, especially when you're also working through trauma, healing your nervous system, and managing life. I had to adapt. I stopped trying to re-create a classroom and started adapting the method to our rhythm. I do some works side-by-side with my daughter. I play music from different countries. I present lessons with humor or hide-and-seek if that's what keeps her engaged. It's still Montessori—just our way."

Fatema: Jordanian mother in Saudi Arabia, homeschooling two under four

"Our utility room became our classroom—it's a tiny corner, but it's ours. I close the door on it when we're not using it to keep the excitement fresh. I used to think Montessori had to be this wide-open space with light wood and baskets. But what really helped me was realizing I could adapt it to what I had. Some days I work on the floor with my baby beside me. Some days we skip it altogether because life takes over. The flexibility to still be Montessori through all of that is what keeps me going."

To learn more about the families featured throughout this book, you'll find their bios in the appendix.

22 | Fostering Independence Through Practice

Releasing Control, Building Capability

> "We must help the child to act for himself, will for himself, think for himself; this is the art of those who aspire to serve the spirit."
>
> —*Dr. Maria Montessori*

Independence is not a milestone—it's a relationship. A process. A series of moments where the child is trusted, supported, and invited to step into their own capacity.

Yet, in practice, this can feel complicated. Because independence is messy. It's slower. It often requires more preparation from the adult, not less. And perhaps most challenging—it requires us to surrender and decenter ourselves.

In Montessori homeschooling, fostering independence isn't just about setting up a self-care station or letting your child crack eggs. It's about seeing the child as capable, even when things take longer, or get louder, or spill. It's about embracing the work behind the work—tying the shoes, slicing the banana, zipping the coat—not once, but dozens of times.

Repetition isn't a separate topic here—it's the invisible thread. It's how independence is formed. Not through a single "I did it!" moment, but through practice. Through *trying again*.

So, when your child insists on pouring the water themselves for the fifth time—or wiping the table even though you could do it faster—remember: this is the curriculum. These are the moments where responsibility is built in real time.

At the heart of it all is the prepared adult who is patient enough to wait, observant enough to know when to step back, and wise enough to see these tiny acts of care as the foundations of lifelong autonomy.

The True Meaning of Independence in Montessori

Independence is not just about a child doing things on their own—it's about building the capacity to act with purpose, confidence, and care.

True independence emerges when:

- The environment is prepared to invite autonomy
- The adult extends trust and expects meaningful contribution
- The child receives guidance without interference, with space to practice
- The opportunity for repetition is honored—because mastery takes time

Montessori does not value independence for its own sake. We value it because it nurtures confidence, develops executive functioning, and prepares the child for real life—not just in the classroom, but in the world.

Independence and responsibility grow together. When a child is invited to care for themselves, their environment, and their community in meaningful ways, they begin to understand: *My actions matter. I am capable. I belong.*

Three Kinds of Independence in Montessori

Dr. Montessori said that independence is not one-dimensional—it develops across multiple domains, each supporting the child's growth into a capable, responsible, human being.

The three core types of independence are:

- **Physical independence:** The ability to care for one's body and surroundings—dressing, toileting, preparing food, and cleaning up. This is often the first kind of independence we observe, especially in the early years.
- **Mental independence:** The capacity to think critically, make choices, solve problems, and initiate work. This grows as the child is given freedom within clear limits, and learns to trust their own thinking.
- **Emotional and moral independence:** The ability to self-regulate, express needs with clarity, and take ownership of behavior. This is where self-discipline takes root—and where the adult's modeling matters most.

Each of these forms of independence is nurtured through daily life, not direct instruction. The child doesn't need a lecture on "how to be independent"—they need the opportunity to practice independence in a developmentally appropriate, prepared environment.

Our task as Montessori adults is to observe closely, step back intentionally, and step in wisely—always asking: *What kind of support does this moment call for?*

This is the art of guiding without controlling. And it's how true independence is born.

Setting the Stage: Creating a Montessori Home Environment That Supports Independence

Independence doesn't emerge from expectations—it emerges from invitation. And the environment is the invitation.

A child cannot thrive in independence if their world is built solely for adults. A Montessori home reimagines the environment so that children can care for themselves, contribute to daily life, and build real capability—little by little, with dignity.

Set Up Self-Care Stations   True independence begins with self-respect. That means giving children access to what they need to care for their own body. Not in theory—in practice.

Start small and keep it functional. A self-care station should be accessible, calming, consistent.

Examples:

- A low mirror with a basket containing a hairbrush, cloth, and tissues
- A mini handwashing station with a pitcher, bowl, towel, and soap
- A simple wardrobe with two to three outfit choices at their level
- A toileting area with wipes, toilet paper, and a change of clothes in reach

These spaces aren't there to push the child—they're there to *make independence possible*. If your child asks for help, that's normal. Independence grows through practice, not pressure.

Embed Practical Life in Your Daily Rhythm   Montessori doesn't separate "real life" from "school life." Practical life is not merely a curriculum box to check—it's the curriculum of childhood. It's the child's training ground for responsibility, order, and confidence.

This means we don't assign chores like arbitrary tasks, and we don't ask for help as though it's optional. The truth is always in the middle. Instead, we integrate the child into the work of the home in a way that feels meaningful and developmentally appropriate.

Invite your child to contribute, not assist. Here's what that looks like:

- "It's time to sweep after snack. I'll do under the table—you do near the chairs."
- "Please wash the blueberries and place them in a bowl so we're ready for snack."
- "Dinner is ready—please help set the table."
  Your child can contribute in many ways, including:
- Preparing simple meals (slice fruit, stir batter, spread butter)
- Cleaning their environment (sweep, wipe, fold)
- Caring for plants and pets

- Packing their own bag for outings
- Helping with laundry and dishes

These aren't chores—they're opportunities for responsibility, order, and pride. They're contributions to shared life. When we normalize participation from a young age, we don't have to convince the child to help—they already see themselves as someone who contributes.

And remember: it only works if the environment supports it. Provide tools that fit their hands, a step stool to reach the counter, and a rhythm that allows space for repetition. Independence can't be rushed—but it can be beautifully supported.

Use Language That Builds Trust and Ownership The way we speak to our children becomes their inner voice. Montessori adults choose words that reflect confidence in the child—not criticism or shame.

Instead of, "You need to be more responsible," try:

- "I trust you with this."
- "You are learning to take care of your things."
- "You can try again."
- "Would you like help setting up a system?"

Instead of, "you always forget," try:

- "Let's figure out what would help you remember."

Responsibility is not imposed—it's modeled, supported, and spoken into being. Your words shape the child's self-perception. Choose them with care.

Letting Go of Perfection: When Independence Gets Messy

One of the greatest barriers to independence isn't the child—it's our own attachment to how things *should* look. We crave control. Clean counters. Quick transitions. Predictable outcomes. But Montessori reminds us: *learning is a process, not a performance.*

Real independence is bumpy. It's uneven. It's slower, messier, and sometimes downright inconvenient. But that's not the problem—it's the point.

This means:

- Letting the child pour their own water—even if they spill
- Letting them choose their outfit—even if it clashes
- Letting them wipe the table—even if crumbs remain
- Letting them crack the egg—even if some shell gets in

None of this is a setback. It's the curriculum.

Perfection is not the goal—*ownership is.* When we allow children to practice without rushing in to correct every imperfection, we send a powerful message: I trust you to keep learning. And that trust is what builds responsibility.

As Montessori adults, our work is not to make things flawless—but to make them *possible.* That means preparing our spaces and our hearts for what real learning looks like: effortful, imperfect, and deeply worth it.

What Independence Looks Like in the Homeschool Work Cycle

When you begin homeschooling, your child will likely need you as a consistent partner throughout the entire work cycle. Expect this. Especially in the early years, independence isn't automatic—it's nurtured over time through support, structure, and trust.

For the primary child, independence often means working alongside you, not apart from you. They'll want your presence, your affirmation, your collaboration. In these moments, your role is more like a peer—quietly supporting without directing, showing up with calm consistency. This is not the time to center your own to-do list. It's about building the trust that will one day lead to separation.

As your child enters the elementary years, you'll begin to see a shift. They'll start taking more ownership—moving between lessons, extending their work, solving problems on their own. You'll still be needed, but in bursts, not constantly. This stage is where independence and responsibility deepen. By upper elementary, the balance tips—your child spends more time working independently than with you. And you may find yourself missing those early days of side-by-side collaboration.

By adolescence, that independence will be fully in bloom. Your role becomes more of a consultant than a co-worker—available, supportive, but not in the mix moment-to-moment.

This is the arc of Montessori: from dependence to collaboration to independence. We are in it for the long term—not for compliance or convenience, but for growth. Adjust your expectations accordingly. Independence doesn't happen because you demand it. It happens because you prepare for it, model it, and allow it to unfold through repetition and trust.

Practical Reminders for Supporting Independence

- Observe first. What is your child ready for?
- Say yes more. If your child shows interest in helping—let them.
- Use real tools. Children feel more capable with real, functioning items sized for their use.
- Rotate responsibilities. What they resist one week, they may embrace the next.
- Keep a "yes shelf." A small area where everything is 100% child-approved and accessible without help.
- Model care for self and environment. They're watching you, always.
- Slow down. Rushing is the enemy of independence.
- Reflect. Is this task actually urgent? Or am I prioritizing convenience over growth?

Independence Begins with Trust

Responsibility isn't something we can lecture into the child. It isn't built by reminding them what they "should" be doing. It's built in the moment we step back and let them try.

Independence is not something we give—it's something we *prepare for*. We model it. We make it possible. And most of all, we allow it to unfold—even when it's slower, messier, or less efficient than doing it ourselves.

So, the next time your child reaches to help, insists on doing it "by myself," or asks to try something new . . .

Pause.

Instead of saying "Not right now," or "Let me do it," consider what you're really being asked: *Can you trust me with this?*

Say yes—when you can.

Give them time. Give them the tools. But most importantly, give them your trust. Because that trust is the foundation of independence. And that's how we raise self-reliant, thoughtful, capable human beings—one small act of responsibility at a time.

Thoughts from the Frontlines

Independence in Montessori isn't the end goal—it's the result of patient practice. It's built through repetition, trust, and tiny opportunities to try again. In this chapter, we see how real families foster responsibility by preparing the environment, stepping back, and letting their children grow through experience.

Wennie: Part-time nurse, Montessori homeschooling in a small apartment

"The rhythm of our day and the structure of our environment is what allows independence to grow. I use a visual calendar for my non-reader so he knows what to expect. I have preset audio cues—like a gentle chime for getting ready to leave the house—so I don't have to be the one nagging. They learn what needs to happen and begin to do it themselves, bit by bit. It's not just about teaching them to be independent; it's about setting them up to succeed."

Viviana: Romanian-Albanian mother of three, Montessori after virtual school

"At first, my daughter had no idea how to choose for herself. In kindergarten, everything had been dictated. Even with the freedom to choose, she'd sit and wait for me to tell her what to do. I had to re-teach independence. I gave her gentle reminders, modeled choices, praised her when she made decisions—and then let her practice. It took time, but now she moves through her routine and shelf work with so much more confidence. It's not perfect, but it's definitely working."

Wilka: Puerto Rican-Filipino mom, working part-time while homeschooling

"We started small—choosing clothes, setting up her snack bag, vacuuming after dinner. My daughter thrives on ownership, so I try to let her know how much I trust her. When she forgets something, we talk through it without shaming. I love how Montessori views mistakes: they're not failures, they're part of the process. That's exactly how we approach independence in our home. And I remind myself too—it's not a single lesson. It's daily practice, for both of us."

To learn more about the families featured throughout this book, you'll find their bios in the appendix.

23 | Montessori Discipline and Conflict Resolution

Leading with Boundaries and Respect

Let's be honest—when most people hear the word discipline, they think of control. Correction. Punishment. The kind of adult-imposed consequence designed to "teach a lesson."

But in Montessori, the lesson is not taught through fear or compliance. It's lived. Repeated. Modeled. And eventually, internalized.

True discipline—the kind we care about in Montessori—is not something done *to* a child. It's something that develops *within* them. Through purposeful activity. Through responsibility. Through repeated opportunities to make a choice and experience its consequences.

Dr. Maria Montessori called this *internal discipline,* and it is one of the central aims of all her work.

Discipline Is the Whole Point of Montessori

Let's start with a foundational reminder: the point of Montessori is not to create a perfect shelf or a child who can recite the continents.

Montessori is a long-term, character-building solution—not a compliance one. The point is to support the child in becoming a self-directed, self-aware, socially responsible human being—someone who chooses to do the right thing, not because they're afraid of punishment, but because they *want* to.

That doesn't happen by accident. It's cultivated. Slowly. Carefully. Consistently. Montessori discipline is rooted in the prepared environment, the prepared adult, clear expectations, and meaningful work. It's not about control—it's about clarity, follow-through, and trust.

Self-Discipline vs. Self-Direction

There's a lot of talk about self-directed learning in Montessori, and unfortunately, that term is often misunderstood. Self-direction is not the same as simply "letting the child choose." And self-discipline doesn't magically emerge because you've created a beautiful space.

Let's clarify:

- **Self-directed learning** means the child is able to choose meaningful, purposeful work that is appropriate to their stage of development— and they know how to move through the work cycle with increasing independence. But this only happens after they've received clear presentations, had opportunities for repetition, and experienced a consistent structure that supports choice.
- **Self-discipline** is the inner development that allows the child to follow through on those choices with focus, care, and respect for the materials, the environment, and others. It's not something we teach directly—it's something that emerges over time through internal growth, supported by rhythm, order, and adult modeling.

In the First Plane of Development (ages 0-6), children are not capable of full self-direction. They are still in a sensitive period for order, movement, and language, and their ability to make purposeful choices is still forming. That's why our role is so crucial: We don't sit back and hope self-discipline appears. We help them move toward independence by preparing the environment, offering freedom with clear boundaries, modeling respectful behavior, and providing a predictable structure.

Self-direction and self-discipline are goals, not starting points. And in Montessori, we help children reach those goals by meeting them exactly where they are—developmentally, emotionally, and neurologically.

Confusing Discipline with Control

Montessori is not permissive. It's deeply principled. We do not cater every lesson to a passing interest or allow disorder in the name of freedom. But we also don't rely on punishments, bribes, or arbitrary rules to enforce behavior. Instead, we guide children through consistent expectations, logical consequences, and trust in their developmental

Here's the distinction:

- *Compliance* means doing what you're told to avoid punishment or to please authority. It's external, short-term, and adult-centered.
- *Obedience* in Montessori is internal. It arises as the child develops concentration, coordination, and will—foundations built over time through modeling, repetition, and clear limits.

Example: A child spills water while pouring.

- **Traditional model:** The adult might step in immediately—scolding or fixing it for the child.
- **Permissive model:** The spill might be ignored entirely.
- **Montessori model:** The child is calmly guided to clean it up on their own. No shame. No reward. Just responsibility supported with dignity.

We prepare the environment for self-regulation, rather than relying on correction. And this is how real discipline develops—from within. The goal is to help them learn to control themselves—with increasing confidence and connection. This takes time, modeling, and trust—in ourselves and in our children.

Your Job Is Not to Make the Child Happy

It's tempting to believe—especially as homeschooling parents—that if our child is frustrated it's a sign of failure. That if they resist, cry, or say, "I don't like this," something is wrong. That we've made a mistake and should abandon the plan to try something new.

But here's the truth: frustration is part of learning. Your job is not to keep your child happy. Montessori doesn't shield children from challenge—it prepares them to face it with increasing resilience. Your role isn't to prevent every moment of discomfort. Your role is to recognize that struggle can be productive, and that limits—when offered with calm authority—are a gift.

Yes, your child will test boundaries. They will push back against limits. They may cry, protest, and disengage. That's not a signal to change the expectation. It's a sign that they are learning to meet it. Your job is to stay steady. To remain the sage, anchored adult who protects the integrity of the work—even when it's hard. To guide without rescuing, and to lead without overpowering.

This is how we build trust. This is how we develop real internal discipline. This is how we raise children who are not just happy—but capable.

Clarity Is Kindness

Children thrive when expectations are clear, consistent and calmly held. What creates anxiety and misbehavior isn't structure—it's inconsistency. Guessing what the adult wants. Feeling unsure about what comes next, or what will happen if a boundary is crossed.

This is where Montessori shines. You offer freedom within limits—and those limits are clear, firm, and fair.

- "You may choose any work you've been shown, and you must return it to the shelf when you're done."
- "You may express how you feel, and you may not hurt others or throw materials."
- "You may take a break, but we're still responsible for caring for our space."

This isn't authoritarian. It's authoritative. The difference? Authoritarian adults lead with control and manipulation. Permissive adults avoid limits. Authoritative adults lead with warmth, clarity, and consistency. Montessori teaches us that true freedom is found within structure—not the absence of it.

When children can trust that the adult means what they say—and follows through without anger or chaos—they feel safe. And safety is what allows them to explore, take risks, and grow.

Natural and Logical Consequences

In Montessori, we avoid rewards and punishments. Not because we're permissive, but because we want children to learn responsibility from the reality of their choices. We're not aiming for obedience rooted in fear. We're aiming for awareness, accountability, and ultimately—self-regulation.

Natural consequences are what happen without interference:

- You forget your hat, and your head gets cold.
- You throw the water, and your work is too wet to continue.

Logical consequences are adult-guided outcomes directly connected to the behavior:

- You throw the pitcher; we put it away until you're ready to use it safely.
- You yell in the reading corner; you're invited to return when you can respect the quiet space.

In both cases, the consequence is:

- Related to the behavior
- Respectful to the child
- Focused on learning, not shame

This approach teaches children *how* to think—not *what* to think. It reinforces that actions have outcomes, and that we're here to support—not control—their growth into responsible, capable humans.

Real-Life Scenarios

Let's make this practical.

Scenario 1: Your child is throwing materials. Instead of saying, "Stop it!" or punishing, you calmly intervene. "These materials are for careful work. I'm going to put them away now. We can try again later."

If this happens repeatedly, reintroduce the material, offer a Grace and Courtesy lesson, or observe to see if the material is too challenging or overstimulating.

Scenario 2: Your child refuses to clean up. Stay grounded and say. "In our home, we all clean up after our work. Would you like to clean it now or after snack?" If they still refuse, say, "I see you're having a hard time. I'll set a timer for five minutes, and then we'll work together to clean up."

Scenario 3: Your child says "no" to everything. Calmly assess whether they need fewer choices, more rest, or clearer expectations. Then offer, "You may choose pouring or transferring. If you're not ready to choose, I'll choose for you this time."

Grace and Courtesy as Preventative Discipline

Montessori conflict resolution starts long before conflict occurs.

Grace and Courtesy lessons—like how to ask for a turn, how to say excuse me, or how to express frustration respectfully—build the social–emotional foundation children need to self-regulate. Practice these in neutral moments. Use role-play. Keep them short, fun, and consistent. Think of them as the "preventative care" of Montessori discipline.

Repetition Is Part of the Process

If you find yourself repeating the same boundary 10 times—welcome. That's not failure. That's childhood. Discipline doesn't happen in one conversation. It's cultivated through repeated experiences of:

- Clear boundaries
- Predictable follow-through
- Loving, calm presence

Children are learning through every interaction. You don't need to be perfect. You just need to be prepared and consistent.

Guiding Toward Responsibility

In the end, your role is not to force your child into compliance—it's to lead them toward *ownership*. That's what self-discipline looks like.

You lead by example. You guide with clarity. You allow space for effort, mistakes, and growth. And in doing so, you raise a child who can make thoughtful choices, repair missteps, and act with integrity.

Montessori discipline isn't soft- it's steady. It's not permissive or punitive—it's principled. It doesn't seek momentary compliance—it cultivates *lifelong responsibility*. That's why it's not easy. And that's why it works.

You are not just teaching your child how to behave—you're helping them become who they are meant to be. Discipline is not a separate subject, it's not something we do outside of our work cycles—it's the heartbeat of our work. For them. And for us.

Thoughts from the Frontlines

In Montessori, discipline isn't about control—it's about building internal awareness, emotional regulation, and responsible decision-making. Through structure, consistency, and modeling, children learn to navigate conflict and consequences with clarity and trust. This chapter explores how discipline is built in real homes, not through punishment, but through presence, boundaries, and connection.

Mae-Lin: U.S. Army veteran and trauma-informed Montessori parent

"Early on, I realized I was reacting more than I was responding. I wanted compliance, but what I really needed was connection. When I felt myself getting triggered, I started naming it: 'I'm angry right now and need to take a moment'. I would leave the room, come back regulated, and model emotional recovery. That moment became a lesson—not in obedience, but in emotional intelligence. Discipline in our home now means holding firm boundaries while holding space for her big feelings. It's taken inner work, but it's changed everything."

(continued)

(continued)

Sarah: Homeschooling mom of four on a hobby farm

"With four kids, there's always someone upset, interrupting, or pushing back. What's helped the most is consistency and clarity—everyone knows what the expectations are. And when there's conflict, we treat it as part of the day. Sometimes I'll stop and we'll have a grace and courtesy lesson right there: how to interrupt politely, how to decline respectfully, how to share space. We also talk about natural consequences. If someone doesn't do their job, we discuss how it impacts the family. It's not a punishment—it's a conversation."

Fatema: Former engineer, homeschooling her toddler and baby in Saudi Arabia

"Some days it feels like the chaos is bigger than me—two little ones, emotions flying. What keeps me grounded is returning to purpose. If my son gets upset or refuses something, I try to pause, observe, and think: what's really going on here? I've learned not to judge his behavior as 'bad' right away. Montessori helped me shift from reaction to understanding. Even when I have to hold a boundary, I do it with empathy: 'I see you're upset. I'm here. We'll try again'. That kind of discipline has brought peace to our home."

To learn more about the families featured throughout this book, you'll find their bios in the appendix.

24

Fostering Concentration and Focus

The Path to Normalization: Supporting Deep Work Through Clear Expectations and Intentional Practice

If there's one quality every homeschool parent wishes they could bottle and sprinkle throughout the day, it's focus. One moment your child is fully engaged, and the next, they're upside down on the couch or asking to switch activities before the first is even underway.

It can be easy to assume something's wrong. But in Montessori, concentration isn't forced or scheduled. It's cultivated. And like all meaningful growth, it takes time, repetition, and trust.

Dr. Maria Montessori famously said, "The first essential for the child's development is concentration. The child who concentrates is immensely happy." That joy doesn't come from completing a checklist. It comes from the deep satisfaction of meaningful engagement.

This chapter explores what concentration looks like in a Montessori home, how to support it, and why your role as the prepared adult matters more than you think.

What Concentration Really Looks Like

We often associate concentration with silence and stillness, but in early childhood, it can be active, repetitive, and yes—a little noisy. A toddler scooping rice over and over? That's concentration. A preschooler rebuilding the same tower 10 times with slight variations? Also concentration. The key isn't to demand stillness. It's to prepare the environment and allow time for engagement to unfold.

Ask yourself:

- Is this material interesting and developmentally appropriate?
- Have I given them enough uninterrupted time to get into a flow?
- Is the environment calm and orderly?

The Development of Concentration: A Timeline

It's helpful to understand that concentration builds over time—and in different ways at each age.

Ages 0–3: Building the Foundation   At this stage, focus is fragile and momentary. Infants and toddlers concentrate through movement and repetition. A toddler might repeat a simple task like putting on socks or pouring water over and over—and that *is* the work.

Your job:

- Offer practical life tasks they can do independently.
- Avoid interrupting when they're deeply engaged—even if it's not what you planned.
- Limit background noise and overstimulation.

Ages 3–6: Strengthening the Skill   Now you'll see more sustained engagement—especially if the child chooses the work. This is the "sensitive period" for order, repetition, and coordination. Disruption is still a major threat to focus at this age, which is why the uninterrupted three-hour work cycle is so critical.

Your job:

- Protect concentration by reducing unnecessary comments or redirections.
- Observe silently when your child is engaged.
- Help them complete the cycle of work (choosing, engaging, restoring).

Ages 6–9: Expansion and Intellectual Focus   Children begin developing "intellectual curiosity"—asking deep questions, following long work sequences, and diving into big ideas. They can hold focus longer but may still struggle with distractions, especially emotional or social ones.

Your job:

- Support big work projects and emerging interests.
- Create systems for organization (journals, checklists, work plans).
- Acknowledge when their energy dips and help them recalibrate.

TIP   Be mindful of your child's stage of development and their sensitivities. This will support you in understanding how to best meet their needs to keep them engaged.

How to Support Concentration at Home

This section explores concrete strategies to help your child focus, without micromanaging their every move.

Protect the Uninterrupted Work Cycle   This is the single most important strategy in Montessori. The three-hour uninterrupted work cycle is not rigidly timed but protected from avoidable disruptions. It allows your child to:

- Explore freely
- Return to work multiple times
- Settle into their rhythm without being redirected

TIP   Avoid asking questions like "Do you want to do this?" in the middle of work time. Hold space quietly, observe, and trust the process.

Minimize Environmental Distractions   Children cannot filter sensory input the way adults do. Background noise, clutter, screens, bright lights, and even busy patterns can impact their ability to focus.

Try this:

- Turn off the TV or radio during work time.
- Limit visual clutter in your homeschool space.
- Keep the number of materials on the shelf manageable—less is more.

Build Transitions Around Anchors   Many children struggle with switching gears. If your child resists starting work or melts down when it's time to clean up, they may need more predictable transitions.

Use consistent cues like:

- A song or chime to start or end work
- A visual schedule
- A transition object (a work rug, a basket)

You can also give a *heads-up*: "In five minutes, we'll wrap up and choose one more work."

Offer the Right Challenge   If your child seems "distracted" or if they are avoiding work, it may be that the material is too difficult—or not difficult enough. Most often, too difficult—not necessarily academically. The work might be difficult because there are too many steps, or perhaps you talked too much during a lesson and you confused the purpose of the work or confused the child.

Ask yourself:

- Does this activity offer repetition with variation?
- Is it too familiar or too complex?
- Can I offer a new presentation or revisit a foundational lesson?

- Did I stick to the aim of the material or did I go off on a tangent when I was giving this lesson?
- Was the lesson interrupted several times?

"A child who is deeply challenged (but not overwhelmed) will often re-enter flow."

Common Challenges and What to Do

Scenario 1: "My child jumps from work to work without finishing anything"

This is normal in the early weeks or when concentration hasn't yet stabilized. Instead of labeling it as a problem, observe.

- Are they exploring or avoiding?
- Are they mimicking what they've seen, or testing limits?
- Have you modeled completing the cycle of work?

Strategy: Give one clear expectation, like "Choose one work and restore it before choosing another." Be patient and consistent.

Scenario 2: "They just want to play instead of doing lessons"

Play is how children process what they've learned. Don't treat it as separate from learning.

Try this:

- Observe the kind of play they're gravitating toward. It may inform your next presentation.
- Use play as an entry point into work ("You were building so carefully. Want to try the red rods next?").

Scenario 3: "My child can't focus unless I sit right next to them"

You may be anchoring their attention. That's okay—but over time, the goal is independence.

Try this:

- Sit beside them silently during work, but don't direct.
- Gradually increase your distance while staying present in the room.
- Let them know, "I'm nearby, and I believe you can do this."

Letting Go of Perfect Focus

It's tempting to measure progress by how long your child concentrates or how much they "get done." But Montessori invites you to let go of perfection and lean into presence.

Some days will feel smooth. Others will be filled with restlessness. That doesn't mean your child isn't learning. It means they're human—and so are you.

Your job is not to force focus, but to:

- Protect it when it appears
- Model it in your own life
- Trust that it will deepen over time

"The child who concentrates is immensely happy." Let that be your guide—not the clock, not the checklist, not the outcome.

The Long Game: What Normalization Really Means

Dr. Montessori called the process of developing concentration, order, and independence *normalization*.

Normalization is not about children behaving perfectly or sitting quietly for hours. It's about reaching a place of peaceful, self-directed engagement. It's when your child finds joy in purposeful work and returns to it again and again.

Normalization doesn't happen through reward charts or rigid schedules. It happens when children:

- Engage in meaningful work
- Repeat it without interruption
- Experience the pride of mastery

And none of that happens overnight. It takes patience. Preparation. And presence. Focus isn't a finish line—it's a relationship. One you build together, day by day.

In the conclusion, you'll explore what it means to embrace the Montessori lifestyle, reflect on your journey, and continue forward with confidence and clarity.

Thoughts from the Frontlines

Concentration is often misunderstood as stillness or silence—but in Montessori, it's about deep, purposeful engagement. Whether a child is carefully spooning beans or building a complex sentence with the movable alphabet, the focus lies in their connection to the work. This chapter explores how real homeschool parents prepare their environments, adjust expectations, and support their child's evolving relationship with concentration.

Wennie: Nurse and part-time homeschooling mom of two in a small apartment

"We live in a small space, so we had to get intentional fast. I learned early that focus doesn't just happen—it has to be prepared for. I keep our learning space free of clutter, play soft instrumental music during the work cycle, and only put out materials they've had a lesson on. I also set visual and audio cues: a biweekly picture calendar for my non-reader, a chime when it's time to tidy, and consistent rhythms throughout the day. Concentration began to grow when everything in the environment supported it—including me being fully present."

Wilka: Part-time working mom of one in a multilingual household

"I used to expect my daughter to focus immediately, especially after I'd spent so much time preparing a lesson. But I've learned that concentration comes in waves. What's helped most is setting up our environment with just the right amount of work on the shelf and soft piano music playing. When she's in flow, I step back. When she's

(continued)

(continued)

distracted, I gently guide her back to the expectation: 'This work cycle is your time—how would you like to use it?' I'm learning that my calm, steady presence is just as important as any material."

Julianne: Montessori DIYer and minimalist mom in Northern Ireland

"We separated the play space from the learning space, and it made a huge difference in concentration. My daughter knew the learning space was for focus. We also implemented a visual routine chart and a clear structure to our day—she thrives on knowing what comes next. But I had to work on myself too. I used to interrupt her thinking without realizing it, or I'd jump in too quickly to 'help'. Now, I sit quietly, take notes, and let her struggle a bit. That's when I see the spark of real concentration—when she figures it out for herself."

To learn more about the families featured throughout this book, you'll find their bios in the appendix.

Conclusion: What's Next

Embracing the Lifestyle, Preparing for the Long Game

You've made it to the final chapter—and that in itself is worth celebrating!

You've spent hours reading, reflecting, observing, and preparing. You've sat with hard questions, rearranged your space, and reimagined what education could look like—not just for your child, but for your whole family. That kind of intention is rare. It's powerful. It matters.

But this isn't the end of your Montessori journey. It's the beginning.

Montessori isn't a checklist to complete or a finish line to cross. It's a way of living—a method rooted in presence, trust, and transformation. It changes the way you see your child, your home, and yourself. And once you start living this way, you won't want to go back.

There Is No Final Destination

There is no perfect curriculum. No flawless implementation. No "right" pace. There's only this:

The steady, ongoing work of preparing yourself, observing your child, and responding to what life is asking of you right now.

There will be seasons of flow—when your child works with joy and independence, and it feels like everything is clicking. And there will be seasons of resistance, boredom, transition, or challenge—when you're unsure if anything is working.

Montessori can hold *all* of it—*if you let go of the idea that it has to look a certain way to be valid.*

> **TIP**   *You don't need more information—you need integration.* By now, you've probably realized something important: You don't need another curriculum right now. You don't need more printables or Pinterest inspiration. What you need is the confidence to apply what you already know. To trust what you've practiced. To live what you've learned.

Montessori doesn't live in the materials. It lives in the way you show up. It's not about *knowing more*. It's about *noticing more*. Pausing more. Reacting less. Refining your rhythm. Returning to your observations.

You've already done the hardest part—you began. You made the courageous choice to walk a different path—not because it was easy, but because it felt right. Now, the work is about sustaining that choice with intention.

It's about choosing consistency over comparison, process over perfection, presence over performance. It's about returning to what you've learned—again and again—each time with deeper understanding.

How to Know the Method Is Working

It won't always feel obvious. You won't always have neat outcomes to point to. But look for these signs:

- Your child repeats work because they want to—not because you told them to.
- They begin to show pride in their independence—wiping their own spills, sweeping the floor, helping a sibling.
- They ask better questions. They linger longer at their work.
- They initiate learning.
- And you, too, are changing—you observe more, react less, and feel more present in the moment.

These are the signs. They may not appear in a test score or a transcript. But they are proof of authentic learning—the kind that lasts.

You Are the Method

You've heard it throughout this book: *The adult is part of the prepared environment.* That's not poetic fluff. That's developmental science.

It's in the way you declutter—not just your shelves, but your expectations. It's in the way you model grace, curiosity, and flexibility. It's in the way you slow down to *really* see your child.

Dr. Maria Montessori said, "The child is both a hope and a promise for mankind." But she also said, "The first thing required of a teacher is that he be rightly disposed."

> "Montessori works best when the adult is also transforming."

You don't need to know everything. You just need to keep becoming the kind of adult who can guide without controlling, observe without rushing, and prepare without perfection. You are not "just" a parent. You are not "just" homeschooling. *You are the prepared adult.* And that is the most powerful curriculum your child could ever have.

Stay Grounded in a Noisy World

There will be noise. Comparison. Doubt. You'll be tempted to question your rhythm, wonder if your child is "behind," and fear you're not doing enough.

When that happens, come back to your *why*. Come back to your child. Come back to your observations.

Let your next step be guided not by fear, but by clarity. Not by urgency, but by purpose. Not by productivity, but by presence.

If You're Ready to Go Deeper

This book is just the beginning. If you want to continue the work, here's how to stay rooted:

- **Keep observing:** Your child will tell you what they need—without words—if you know how to watch.
- **Revisit this book:** What feels obvious now might hold new depth in a few months.

- **Join community:** Whether online or in person, don't do this alone. Mentorship and connection matter much more than you think.
- **Take a course made for Homeschoolers:** You don't need classroom training—it was never designed for the homeschool context. You're guiding across all planes of development, not just one. If there's one truth to take from this book, it's this: we are all shaped by our environments. And the home environment is fundamentally different from a classroom.
  - Consider *The Montessori Homeschool Academy*™—a comprehensive course with guided coaching and a global community of learners. It focuses on your preparation as the adult, not just what lessons to teach, but how to lead with integrity and high-fidelity to the method at home.
- **Stay humble. Stay curious. Stay grounded:** The best guides are lifelong learners. You will overcorrect. You will fall into old habits. But each time you return, you return stronger. This is a work of constant recalibration.

Montessori for Life

This was never about checking boxes. It was about cultivating connection. It was about aligning your life with your values. It was about choosing a way of learning that lets your child grow whole.

You've done that. You're doing that. And now, you get to keep doing it—one slow, intentional, beautiful day at a time.

You're not at the end. You're at the beginning. From Pinterest-scrolling to prepared adult. From self-doubt to self-trust. From wishing it could be different . . . to making it so. This is your Montessori homeschool. This is your family's education. This is your way of life.

And you are ready.

So go forward—not with fear, but with clarity.

Not with a script, but with a compass.

Not with the need to get it "right"—but with the courage to keep showing up.

Welcome to the next chapter of your journey. Make it an authentic one.

Glossary
of Montessori Terms

Absorbent Mind   A concept developed by Dr. Montessori describing a young child's capacity to take in everything around them effortlessly, especially during the first six years of life. This period is crucial for learning language, movement, and social behaviors.

Activity   In Montessori, an *activity* is a task or exercise designed with a specific developmental purpose. Each activity encourages learning through hands-on engagement and is often presented to children as a lesson or demonstration.

Approach   A general way of guiding learning, including overall principles and attitudes (e.g., Montessori's child-centered approach). *See also* method and philosophy.

Assessment (Traditional and Montessori)

Traditional Assessment   Typically refers to evaluating student learning through tests, quizzes, and standardized exams. It often measures knowledge retention and compares performance to set standards or benchmarks.

Montessori Assessment   In Montessori, assessment is ongoing and observational. Rather than tests, guides assess a child's understanding by observing their interactions, engagement, and mastery of materials over time. This approach respects each child's developmental stage and unique learning pace.

Auto-Education (Self-Education)   The concept that children have an innate ability to learn independently. In Montessori, this means creating an environment that encourages children to explore, make discoveries, and reach conclusions on their own, with the adult acting as a guide rather than an instructor.

Beginner (as it applies to this book)   In this context, a beginner is a parent new to Montessori homeschooling, typically unfamiliar with the details of Montessori philosophy, materials, and practices. They are likely eager to learn but may feel overwhelmed by the wealth of information or unsure of where to start.

Constructivism   An educational theory that suggests children construct knowledge through hands-on experience and active exploration. In constructivist learning, children build on previous knowledge by interacting with their environment, rather than passively absorbing information.

Consultant   A professional who provides expert advice in specific areas of Montessori education, such as classroom setup, curriculum alignment, or addressing unique challenges.

Control of Error   A feature in Montessori materials or activities that allows children to assess their work. A control of error may be part of the material itself, or an aspect created by the teacher, encouraging children to observe and check their progress independently, fostering self-reliance.

Curriculum (Traditional)   A structured plan outlining specific content, skills, and knowledge students are expected to learn, often organized by age or grade level. Traditional curricula are typically standardized, with prescribed lessons and materials.

Cycle of Work/Cycle of Activity   Refers to the complete process a child undergoes when working with an activity: selecting it, engaging with it fully, repeating if desired, and finally returning the materials to their proper place. This cycle supports the development of focus and independence.

Deschooling   A transitional period a child (and often the parent) experiences when shifting from a traditional school environment to homeschooling. Deschooling is not a break from learning—it is a reorientation toward intrinsic motivation, curiosity, and connection. See also *unschooling*.

Didactic Materials   Specially designed learning materials unique to the Montessori method, each targeting a specific skill or concept. Examples include the Pink Tower, the Moveable Alphabet, and the Number Rods.

Directress/Guide The traditional Montessori term for a teacher, emphasizing the role of the adult as a guide who observes, supports, and facilitates the child's learning rather than directly instructing.

Essential Materials Materials in Montessori that introduce core concepts within the Montessori learning trajectory, are used across multiple age ranges, or can serve as building blocks for creating other materials. For example, the Colored Beads introduce math concepts and can be combined to create activities like the Snake Game, serving multiple purposes over time.

Follow the Child A foundational Montessori principle that means observing and understanding each child's developmental needs, interests, and motivations. Following the child involves recognizing their natural inclinations and developmental stages, then adapting the environment and activities to support their growth.

Foundational Foundational concepts, materials, or practices are those that form the base of Montessori education. They are essential for understanding and implementing Montessori at its core and set the stage for further, more advanced learning.

Freedom Within Limits A core Montessori principle that allows children to make choices within a carefully prepared environment. This freedom fosters independence while ensuring that children engage in productive, respectful behavior.

Grace and Courtesy Lessons in practical social behavior that teach children respect for themselves, others, and their environment. These lessons include polite greetings, waiting turns, and using gentle hands.

Guide (Montessori) In Montessori, a guide is an educator who observes, supports, and facilitates each child's learning. Rather than instructing, the guide prepares an environment conducive to exploration, provides lessons at the right developmental moment, and respects the child's autonomy in learning.

Hands-On Learning The Montessori approach emphasizes learning by doing, with children encouraged to engage with materials actively and physically to understand concepts.

Indirect Preparation A method of introducing skills and knowledge that will be needed for future learning, without explicitly teaching those skills. For example, tracing shapes with fingers prepares children for writing by strengthening fine motor control.

Instructional Coaching   A supportive, collaborative process where an experienced educator works with teachers to improve their instructional practices based on goals. In Montessori, instructional coaching may focus on refining lesson presentations, enhancing observation skills, and fostering a prepared environment. In homeschooling, an instructional coach can support with effective implementation.

Lesson   In Montessori, a "lesson" is often considered the material itself. A lesson involves a purposeful demonstration of the material or activity that guides the child through a specific concept or skill, serving as a stepping-stone for hands-on engagement with actual materials. The child meets the direct aim (commonly referred to as the objective) of the lesson through experiencing the material itself, rather than as a result of any information provided by the teacher.

MACTE Accreditation   Accreditation by the Montessori Accreditation Council for Teacher Education (MACTE) is a standard of quality that ensures Montessori teacher training programs meet rigorous educational standards. It is recognized by the Montessori community and assures that training aligns with authentic Montessori principles.

Mentorship   An experienced individual supporting another's growth and development in a specific area by means of sharing from personal experience. In Montessori, mentorship helps new guides or homeschooling parents learn from someone seasoned in Montessori philosophy, classroom management, and best practices.

Method   A structured, systematic way of teaching specific content, such as using Montessori materials in a sequence to develop a skill or concept. *See also* approach and philosophy.

Montessori Album/Curriculum/Manual   These terms refer to the same resource: a comprehensive guide that Montessori educators use to implement lessons and activities. Montessori albums, or manuals, contain detailed instructions on presenting materials and activities, along with observations and developmental insights to support children's learning at various stages.

Montessori Teaching   Montessori teachers act as guides, facilitating learning rather than instructing. They observe each child's interests and developmental stage, introducing materials and lessons that allow children to explore and construct their understanding independently. *See also* traditional teaching.

Normalization A Montessori term describing the process by which children develop concentration, self-discipline, and a love of work. Normalization occurs when children are deeply engaged in meaningful, self-chosen activities.

Observation The process by which the adult carefully yet nonjudgmentally watches the child to understand their needs, interests, and developmental stage. Observation informs the adult's guidance and environment setup.

Philosophy The underlying beliefs and values that shape a method or approach. Montessori's philosophy is built on respect for the child, independence, and a prepared environment to support natural development. *See also* approach and method.

Planes of Development Montessori's framework of child development, divided into four stages or "planes" (0–6, 6–12, 12–18, and 18–24 years). Each plane has distinct characteristics and developmental needs that guide Montessori practices.

Practical Life Activities that teach real-world skills, fostering independence, coordination, and responsibility. Practical life tasks include pouring, sweeping, dressing, and self-care, all designed to give children a sense of accomplishment and mastery.

Prepared Adult In Montessori, the prepared adult is an educator or guide who has developed the knowledge, patience, and awareness needed to support children's growth. The prepared adult is attuned to the Montessori philosophy, having practiced observation, understanding developmental needs, and creating a nurturing, respectful environment.

Prepared Environment A carefully organized learning space tailored to the developmental needs of children, with accessible materials and freedom to explore within set boundaries.

Presentation The initial demonstration or introduction of a Montessori activity to a child. The guide presents the activity slowly and clearly, allowing the child to observe before trying it on their own.

Progressive Education An educational philosophy that emphasizes experiential, student-centered learning, where children's interests and real-world applications play a central role. Progressive education promotes inquiry, critical thinking, and hands-on activities, often with a focus on social and emotional development.

Scope and Sequence   A scope and sequence is an organized outline of what topics or skills will be covered (scope) and in what order they will be presented (sequence). In Montessori, a scope and sequence provides a flexible, developmental guide that aligns activities with children's evolving interests and abilities, rather than a rigid, grade-based curriculum.

Self-Corrective Material   A Montessori material designed with built-in feedback that allows children to independently identify and correct their mistakes. Self-corrective materials provide immediate feedback, helping children gain confidence and mastery without the need for adult correction.

Sensitive Periods   Phases in child development when they are especially receptive to certain types of learning, such as language, order, or movement. Montessori environments support these sensitive periods by providing activities that align with children's natural interests.

Sensorial Materials   Montessori materials designed to help children refine their senses, such as sight, sound, touch, taste, and smell. Sensorial materials include items like the Pink Tower and Color Tablets, which isolate and enhance specific sensory experiences.

Teacher Training   Formal education programs designed to prepare individuals to become Montessori guides or teachers. These programs, often MACTE-accredited, cover Montessori philosophy, developmental stages, classroom management, and curriculum presentation for different age levels.

Three-Hour Work Cycle   A period during which children engage in uninterrupted, self-chosen activities, fostering deep concentration and flow. This cycle is a staple in Montessori classrooms and can be adapted to home-schooling routines.

Three-Period Lesson   A technique used to introduce vocabulary and concepts in Montessori. It consists of three steps: naming ("This is. . ."), recognizing ("Show me. . ."), and recalling ("What is this?").

Traditional Education   An education model that often relies on structured, teacher-led instruction, fixed curricula, and standardized assessments. Traditional education typically emphasizes rote memorization, external rewards, and a set sequence of skills based on age or grade level. *See also* Montessori teaching.

Traditional Teaching   Typically involves direct instruction where the teacher conveys information, and students are expected to memorize and reproduce it. Emphasis is often on conformity, control, and external assessment.

Unschooling   A learner-driven approach to education that forgoes structured curricula in favor of a child's natural curiosity and interests. Unschooling trusts that children learn best when they pursue topics that genuinely engage them, with the adult acting as a facilitator rather than a teacher. A term often confused with *deschooling*.

Work   Montessori refers to the child's activities as "work" to honor their engagement and concentration. This term underscores the respect given to children's purposeful efforts and independence.

Work Cycle   The uninterrupted period during which children engage in self-chosen activities. The work cycle allows children to delve deeply into tasks, fostering focus, resilience, and self-motivation.

Zone of Proximal Development (ZPD)   A concept developed by Lev Vygotsky, often applied in Montessori, describing the range of tasks a child can complete with guidance. In Montessori, materials and lessons are introduced within the child's ZPD to challenge and support growth.

Appendix: Meet the Montessori Mamas

Get to know the incredible women whose stories are woven throughout this book. Each brings her own background, rhythm, and reason for choosing Montessori homeschooling. From diverse cultures and career paths to single-parent homes and bilingual households, these mamas are united in their commitment to learning alongside their children.

Destiny
Location: United States
Family: Single mother raising a four-year-old son
Background: Destiny is a full-time work-from-home mama who began homeschooling when her son was just under three. She centers her Montessori practice on African diaspora studies, bilingualism, and collective community care. Destiny brings deep intentionality to her Montessori Homeschool, which is as much about healing and developmental alignment as it is about education.

Fatema
Location: Saudi Arabia
Family: Stay-at-home mom of a three-year-old son and 10-month-old daughter

Background: With a background in engineering and experience working in education in Jordan, Fatema turned to homeschooling as a way to raise her children differently than the cultural norms around her. She's balancing Montessori homeschooling while navigating a toddler-baby combo, self-doubt, and a shifting sense of self—always with honesty, humor, and heart.

Julianne Maria
Location: Northern Ireland
Family: Homeschooling her four-year-old daughter with her husband
Background: Julianne brings Montessori to life in a region where homeschooling is rare. Her family's minimalistic lifestyle, creative spirit, and love of natural learning fuel their days. She also co-runs Moon & Tree Montessori, creating handmade learning materials and advocating for accessible, child-centered education inspired by her homeschool journey.

Mae-Lin
Location: United States
Family: Married mother to one five-year-old daughter
Background: Mae-Lin is a U.S. Army veteran, world traveler, and trauma-informed parent. Mae-Lin's story is one of deep inner work. She approaches Montessori as a path to healing and connection— valuing emotional literacy, personal growth, and conscious parenting just as much as academics.

Maria Isabel
Location: Sweden (originally from Colombia)
Family: Lives with her husband and young son
Background: Originally from Colombia, Maria Isabel lives in Sweden with her husband and son. She began homeschooling after realizing that the local Montessori school lacked alignment with authentic practice. Her trilingual, multicultural home reflects her passion for justice and child-led education.

Sarah

Location: United States

Family: Homeschooling mother of four (ages two to nine)

Background: A mother of four and small hobby farmer, Sarah manages her home, homeschooling rhythm, bookkeeping business duties, and a small hobby farm with grace and grit. With her roots in a Montessori-inspired preschool, she brings practical insight and seasoned structure to multi-age learning at home.

Tiffany

Location: United States (originally from Colombia)

Family: Homeschooling mom of three girls (ages seven, three, and one)

Background: Tiffany came to Montessori as a curious, devoted mother wanting the best for her family. With no prior experience in education, Tiffany leans into Montessori with warmth, openness, and commitment. Her home is primarily Spanish-speaking, and she's guiding her children toward biliteracy with intentionality, joy, and trust in the process.

Viviana

Location: United States (Romanian-Albanian household)

Family: Mother of three girls (ages six, three, and one)

Background: A doctor of nursing who stepped away from her medical career to raise and educate her girls at home, Viviana is also a small business owner and thoughtful observer. Her Montessori journey reflects her commitment to self-directed education, organization, and prioritizing family over convention.

Wennie

Location: Canada

Family: Homeschooling two children (ages five and three) while working part-time

Background: A registered nurse and Montessori mama living in a small apartment, she is deeply thoughtful about rhythm, space, and self-organization. She's committed to sustainable homeschooling and values simplicity, clarity, and purposeful presence.

Wilka

Location: United States (Puerto Rican-Filipino household)

Family: Mom of one daughter, age six

Background: Wilka works part-time while homeschooling and raising her daughter bilingually. Her first year felt like a series of checklists—until she embraced Montessori as a mindset. Now, she focuses on observing, preparing, and creating a truly connected learning environment.

Index

A

absorbent mind, 4, 78
abstract thinking, 81, 101, 102
academic benchmarks, 26
academics, Montessori approach to, 151, 165
accessibility versus preparedness, 91
activities, 4, 27, 92, 100, 108
    Montessori-inspired activities, 179
    socialization activities, 161
adapting Montessori, 177
    individualized vs. personalized
        learning, 180–181
    lifelong journey, Montessori as, 182
    pedagogy, Montessori as, 178–181
    perfection, 181–182
    preparedness, 181–182
    what adapting does mean, 179–180
    what adapting doesn't mean, 178–179
adolescence, Montessori in, 103, 190
adult, 39, 65, 73
    authoritarian, 197
    as co-learner, 68–69
    as creator of prepared environment, 67–68
    curiosity and compassion in
        communication, 41
    as emotional anchor, 66–67
    empathy, navigating common concerns
        with, 41–42
    individualized and personalized for,
        180–181
    as leader and observer, 66

    as mentor, 68
    as observer, 66
    permissive adults, 197
    prepared adult, 9, 20, 50, 66, 130, 176, 179,
        182, 186, 202, 212
    role in traditional education and
        Montessori, 53
    as role model and mentor, 68
    values, starting with, 40–41
    as a work in progress, 69
age to begin Montessori homeschooling, 3, 4
AIM Curriculum, 110, 118
albums, 106–107, 118
    non-linear Montessori albums, 106
    Practical Life album, 112
    teacher-created, 109–110
    training center, 110
alignment, 35, 39, 43, 63
AMI (Association Montessori Internationale),
    110, 111, 118
AMS (American Montessori Society) ,
    110, 111, 118
anchors, 132, 162
    artificial, 130
    building transitions around, 204
    emotional anchor, adult as, 66–67
    natural, 130
    to support transitions, 130
appeal of Montessori homeschooling, 7–9
approach, 34, 36, 81, 97, 162, 179
assessment, 55, 167, 170

authentic Montessori, 5, 18, 20, 56, 170, 183
authoritarian adults, 197
autonomy, Montessori education and, 72, 126

B

beginner Montessorian, 106, 107
  best practices for, 142
  lesson planning as, 142
benchmark, 17, 26, 51, 82, 137, 213
benefits of Montessori homeschooling, 8–9
Binomial Cube, 115, 116
botany, 102
botany/zoology puzzles, 121
boundary-setting moments, 45
Box of Sticks, 120
Brown, Brené, 25
Brown Stair, 121
bulletin boards, 54–55

C

CGMS (Center for Guided Montessori
      Studies), 110, 111
challenges in Montessori homeschooling
  blaming the child instead of the setup,
      158–159
  grace and courtesy, revisiting, 157
  letting go of control, 155–156
  managing resistance/disinterest, 156–157
  offering choices within limits, 157
  transitioning from traditional school, 158
checklists, 15, 16, 42, 152, 159, 202
chemistry, 102
child, 73
  development, 18, 78, 97, 161, 195, 217
  not to be blamed for setup
      challenges, 158–159
child-centric home, 90
Childhood Potential Online Conference, 118
child-inclusive home, 90
child-led learning, 72, 75
  vs. adult-driven learning, 181
clarity, 31–32, 94, 99, 128, 136, 196–197
classroom, 54–55, 61, 91, 95, 119
classroom setting, leaving, 15
Clear, James, 131
coaching, 110

co-learner, adult as, 68–69
collaboration, 43, 74, 79, 81, 103, 142,
      150, 190, 191
Color Tablets, 100
communication, 82, 166
  curiosity and compassion in, 41
  extended family communication, 45
community, 2, 118, 162–163, 212
compassion, 41, 66
complementary curriculum, 140, 142
compliance, 18, 52, 54, 55, 109, 155, 158, 191,
      193, 195, 199
concentration, 60, 96, 98, 136, 149
concentration, development of, 203
  ages 0–3, 202
  ages 3–6, 203
  ages 6–9, 203
  common challenges, 205–206
  normalization, 206–207
concentration at home, supporting, 203
  building transitions around anchors, 204
  environmental distractions, minimizing, 204
  right challenge, offering, 204–205
  uninterrupted work cycle,
      protecting, 203–204
confidence, 24, 29, 45, 100, 136, 143,
      186, 189, 207
connection, beginning with, 147
consistency, 27, 30, 73, 75, 92, 99, 126,
      148–149, 166, 179, 190, 196, 199, 210
constructive choices, making, 72
Constructive Triangles, 120
constructivism, 32
consultant, 118, 142, 151, 190
control, 72, 74, 88, 155
  discipline and, 195–197
  letting go of, 155–156
control of error, 8, 116
conversation, 19, 39, 41–42, 45
  knowing when to pause and revisit, 43–44
coordinated hand, 4
core values, 6, 34, 56, 126–127
cosmic task, 88
courtesy, 44, 100, 138–139, 146, 157, 198, 200.
      See also grace and courtesy
creativity, 7, 171
critical thinking, 18, 57, 81

culture, 34, 91, 101
curiosity, 41, 52, 167
    intellectual, 203
curriculum, 15, 86, 88, 105, 106, 107, 110,
        111, 112, 113, 142, 151, 190
    AIM Curriculum, 110, 118
    all-in-one, 16
    complementary, 140, 142
    one-size-fits-all, xvi
    open-and-go, 28, 107
    and pace, 54
    plug-and-play, xiv, 31, 108, 111
    pre-planned, 24
    standardized curriculum, 52, 109, 111
    standardized packages, 109
    teacher-created albums, 109–110
    training center albums, 110
cycle of work, 148, 203. *See also* three-hour
    work cycle

D

daily rhythm
    embed practical life in, 188–189
    and flow, 86
    strengthening, 149
daily rhythm, creating, xvii, 125
    core values, defining, 126–127
    expectations vs. tasks, 128–130
    leading with presence, not
        pressure, 130–131
    three-hour work cycle, 127–128
    using anchors to support transitions, 130
daily routines, 5
Day 1 of Montessori homeschooling
    grace and courtesy lessons, 146–147
    orienting child to Montessori space, 146
    process over product, importance of, 147
    sample work period flow, 147–148
Decanomial Box, 120
decluttering, 88–90
dedicated workspace, 97
deep concentration, 68, 89
deschooling, 13, 14, 18
    as an active process, 15–16
    experiment, 99
    facilitating vs. teaching, 19
    misconceptions about, 15–16

Montessori paradigm, 17–18
non-negotiability of, 16
observation, 18–19
paradigms, 16–17
patience in, 19
prepared environment, creating, 19
rebuilding from the ground up, 15
traditional schooling, 16
trusting the process, 19
deschooling experiment, 99
developmental milestones, 17, 26, 138
developmental readiness, 54, 81
developmental stages of Montessori, 77, 78
    absorbent mind, 78
    four planes of development, 78–79
    freedom within limits, 82
    mature self, 79
    obstacles, removing, 82–83
    reasoning mind, 79
    sensitive periods, 80–82
    social self, 79
developmental timing of Montessori, 3–4
discipline, 72, 193
    clarity, 196–197
    and control, 195–197
    internal, 193, 196
    preventative discipline, grace and
        courtesy as, 198
    repetition as part of the process, 198
    responsibility, guiding toward, 199
    self-discipline, 7, 18, 88, 97, 103, 187,
        194–195, 199
    as the whole point of Montessori, 194–195
disinterest, 156
DIY Montessori, 116–117, 122

E

early childhood, 109, 202
education, xv, xviii, 5, 7, 14, 16, 18, 23, 24, 26,
        32, 65, 66, 78, 88, 99, 126, 139, 167
elementary years, Montessori subjects in
    geography, 102
    geometry, 102
    history, 102
    physical science and chemistry, 102
    zoology and botany, 102
emotional anchor, adult as, 66–67

emotional and moral independence, 187
emotional environment, 44
emotional life, 161, 162
emotional safety, 44
empathy, navigating common concerns
    with, 41–42
environment, 61, 62, 73, 89, 90, 164
    child-accessible, 5
    developmentally informed, 8
    emotional, 44
    in Montessori, 55
    prepared, 6, 8, 36, 67–68, 73, 87, 180
    in traditional education, 54–55
    of unity, 44–45
environmental distractions, minimizing, 204
essential materials, 104, 120–121
expectations, 147, 154–155
    vs. tasks, 128–130
extended family communication, 45
external timeline, 26

F
facilitating vs. teaching, 19
families
    extended family communication, 45
    real Montessori families, 6
    reasons for homeschool, 7
    struggles in bringing Montessori home, 9
family connections, 4, 8
family culture, 176
family rhythm, 179
fear, 14, 23–24, 26, 29
finances, educational, 42
first plane of development, 3, 26, 78,
    81, 101, 194
flexibility, 18, 21, 178
    and responsibility, 178
    within structure, 128
focus, 97. See also concentration,
    development of
    choosing area of, 93
    intellectual, 203
    letting go of perfect focus, 206
    prioritizing, 148–149
follow the child, 6, 71, 77–78
foundation, building, 202
foundational, 26, 28, 139, 167

fourth plane of development, 79
freedom, 7
freedom within limits, 6, 50, 71, 72, 196
    adult, 73
    child, 73
    components that make it work, 72–74
    environment, 73
    missteps and misunderstandings, 74
    practical strategies to get started, 74–75
frustration, 154, 156, 179, 196

G
geography, 102
geometric cabinet, 120
geometry, 102, 120
Golden Beads, 4, 101, 116, 117, 120
Gottman, John, 41
grace and courtesy
    lessons, 146–147
    as preventative discipline, 198
    in real life, 44
    revisiting, 157
    starting with, 138–139
grade-level standards, 137
group belonging, 81
growth, 24, 66, 71
    long-term, 172
    social-emotional, 161, 164, 166, 198
guide, 53, 60–61, 111, 134, 135, 138

H
hands-on learning, 4
hands-on materials, 56, 134
handwriting worksheets, 66
high-integrity Montessori, 55–56
history, 102
home culture, 2, 139
home environment, 87, 88
    accessibility versus preparedness, 91
    consistent rhythms, establishing, 92
    decluttering as a Montessori
        practice, 88–90
    defining function and purpose in, 90
    focus, choosing area of, 93
    integration, 90–91
    observation, 92

practical life, starting with, 92
real Montessori environment, 92–93
understanding, 92
homeschooling parents, 16, 56, 196
homeschool mission statement, creating, 34
homeschool planning, 85
homeschool space, 35
homeschool work cycle, 190–191
human development, 26, 51, 52–53, 78

I

ideal day, visualizing, 35
idealism, 60, 82
identity and independence, 81
imagination, 81
imperfection, embracing in learning, 189–190
independence in Montessori, 6, 186
    adolescence and, 190
    creating a home environment
        supporting, 187–189
    daily contributions, 188–189
    embracing imperfection, 189–190
    emotional and moral, 187
    kinds of, 187
    mental, 187
    physical, 187
    practical reminders for supporting, 191
    self-care stations, , 188
    trust as foundation of, 191
    trust-building language, 189
    work cycle, 190–191
indirect preparation, 68
individualized vs. personalized learning,
    8, 180–181
indoor work, returning to, 147
Instagram, 37, 92, 96, 123, 142
integration, 90–91, 176
intellectual curiosity, 203
intellectual focus, 203
intentional environment, 9, 57, 85
intentional social rhythm, building, 162
    mixed-age experiences, facilitating, 163
    neighborhood outreach, 163
    nervous system, 164
    organic play opportunities,
        creating, 163–164
    social connections, 164

weekly social rhythm, designing, 163
whole child perspective, 165
internal development, 26, 155
internal discipline, 193, 196
internalized timeline, 26
intrinsic motivation, 137
isolation challenges, 162

L

Land and Water Forms, 121
language, 80, 99, 100–101, 120
    trust-building, 189
Large Continent Puzzle Map, 121
leader and observer, adult as, 66
leadership, 74, 88
learning, xv, xviii, 4, 8, 16, 19, 26, 36, 53–54,
        59–60, 61, 62, 66, 67, 68, 69, 75, 84,
        87, 92, 93, 113, 155, 166
    adult-driven, 181
    child-led, 72, 75, 181
    hands-on, 4
    imperfection, embracing in, 189–190
    individualized vs. personalized, 8, 180–181
    love for, 9
    self-directed, 194
    self-paced, 8, 36
    sensorial, 99, 100, 120
learning curve, 24
learning environment, 7, 66, 72, 96–97,
        99, 146
learning process in traditional education and
        Montessori, 53–54
learning space, Montessori, 95
    adolescence, Montessori in, 103
    creating a purposeful, 96–97
    culture, 101
    first shelves, setting up, 98–99
    geography, 102
    geometry, 102
    history, 102
    language, 100–101
    mathematics, 101
    Montessori subjects in elementary
        years, 102
    Montessori subjects in primary
        years, 100–101
    physical science and chemistry, 102

learning space, Montessori (continued)
  practical life, 100
  self-initiated research and
      follow-up work, 103
  sensorial, 100
  shelf, role of, 97–99
  thematic shelf, 99
  transition shelf, 99
  zoology and botany, 102
lesson planning, 136, 137, 142
lessons. *See* Montessori lessons
letting go of control, 155–156
letting go of perfect focus, 206
letting go of perfection, 189–190
lifelong journey, Montessori as, 46, 68, 182
Lillard, Angeline Stoll, 16
limits, offering choices within, 157. *See also*
      freedom within limits
logical consequences, 195, 197–198
long-term goals, 36, 106
long-term growth, 172
long-term intention, defining, 35–36
long-term memory, 97

M
MACTE accreditation, 110, 119
manuals, 106
mastery, 138
  child's path to, 168–169
  self-mastery, 173
material. *See* Montessori materials
math concepts, 28, 120
mathematical mind, 4
mathematics, 99, 101
mature self, 79
measuring progress in Montessori, 142
memory, long-term, 97
mental independence, 187
mentor, adult as, 68
mentorship, 79, 110, 212
metal insets, 120, 171
method, 8, 31, 50, 179, 211
milestones, 15, 17, 26
mind
  absorbent, 4, 78
  mathematical, 4
  reasoning, 79

mixed-age experiences, facilitating, 163
mixed-age groups, 25
mixed-age interaction, 162, 163
Montessori, Maria, 24, 52, 60, 66, 67, 72, 80,
      91, 117, 193, 202, 211
Montessori, Mario, 52, 62
Montessori: The Science Behind the Genius
      (Angeline Stoll Lillard), 16
Montessori albums, 110, 113
  non-linear, 106
  studying, 118
Montessori-aligned, 56
Montessori-aligned coach/consultant, 142
Montessori-aligned supplements, 122
Montessori at home, 4, 5, 9, 14, 72, 123
Montessori Bells, 121
Montessori certification, 24
Montessori classrooms, 61, 91, 115, 119
Montessori coach, hiring, 118
Montessori Compass, 111
Montessori educator, 16, 23, 26
  balancing homeschooling with everything
      else, 26–27
  child development, Montessori
      approach to, 26
  qualification, 24
  socialization, 25
Montessori freedom, 50, 157
Montessori-inspired, 56, 105
Montessori-inspired activities, 179
Montessori-Inspired Continent Boxes, 101
Montessori-inspired daily rhythm, 127
Montessori-inspired decluttering
      approach, 89
"Montessori-inspired" label, 108
Montessori lessons, 6, 8, 68, 92, 106, 134,
      135, 136, 147
  best practices for beginners, 142
  delivery, step-by-step, 141
  differences from traditional lessons, 137
  grace and courtesy as foundation,
      138–139
  parent's role as guide, 142–143
  planning based on observation and
      readiness, 137–138
  planning for beginners, 142
  practicing before presenting, 140

three-period lesson as core strategy, 139–143
upper elementary, adaptations for, 141–142
Montessori materials, 4, 115, 116
  cost and investment in, 27–29
  cultural, 121
  DIY Montessori, 116–117, 122
  effective use and preparation for, 117–119
  essential materials, 120–121
  language, 120
  math, 120
  new, buying, 121
  nice-to-haves, 121
  secondhand, buying, 121
  sensorial/geometry, 120
  smart material choices, making, 116–117
  sources for, 121–122
  substitutes, 122
  supplement, 122
Montessori method, 5, 31
Montessori paradigm, 17–18
Montessori parenting, 88
Montessori philosophy, 93, 133, 140
Montessori revolution, xv–xviii
Montessori subjects in the elementary
      years, 102
  geography, 102
  geometry, 102
  history, 102
  physical science and chemistry, 102
  zoology and botany, 102
Montessori subjects in the primary years, 100
  culture, 101
  language, 100–101
  mathematics, 101
  practical life, 100
  sensorial, 100
Montessori-supportive household, building, 39
  adults, 39–42
  boundary-setting moments, 45
  curiosity and compassion in
      communication, 41
  defining support and clarifying roles, 43
  empathy, navigating common concerns
      with, 41–42
  grace and courtesy in real life, 44
  knowing when to pause and revisit the
      conversation, 43–44

unity, creating an environment of, 44–45
  values, starting with, 40–41
Montessori Teacher™, 107, 111, 118
Montessori Teacher™ Home Learning
      Library, 118
Montessori Teacher™ Scope & Sequence, 111
Montessori tool, 139–143
Month 1 of Montessori homeschooling
  daily rhythm, strengthening, 149
  refinement, 149–150
  shifting from teacher to guide, 150
moral development, 81
motivation, 2, 6, 31, 55
  and assessment in traditional education and
      Montessori, 56
  intrinsic, 137
motor skills, 66, 169
Moveable Alphabet, 116, 120, 146, 180
movement, 53, 54, 62, 78, 80, 100
multi-year developmental cycles, 26

N

NAMC (North American Montessori
      Center), 110
natural and logical consequences, 197
  grace and courtesy as preventative
      discipline, 198
  real-life scenarios, 198
  repetition, 198
neighborhood forum, 163
nervous system, 30, 46, 70, 75, 158, 164, 183
new Montessori homeschoolers, 24, 71,
      115, 139, 153
new Montessori materials, buying, 121
nice-to-haves, 121
non-linear Montessori albums, 106
normalization, 206–207
number rods, 4, 101, 171

O

obedience in Montessori, 195
observation, 6, 18, 46, 66, 76, 92, 106, 111,
      113, 131, 167, 168
  extensions and variations, role of, 170–172
  getting started with, 170–172
  without intervening, 148

observation (continued)
  long-term growth, 172
  and repetition, 169–170
  and work cycle, 148–149
observation opportunity, 148
observation skills, 216
observer, adult as, 66
obstacles, removing, 82–83
open-and-go curriculum, 28
open-and-go plans, 14
open-and-go programs, 107
open-and-go solution, 18
opportunity, 80, 147, 154, 187
order, 61, 80, 132
ordered intellect, 4
organic play opportunities, creating, 163–164
orientation, 150
orienting child to Montessori space, 146
outdated paradigms, unlearning, 14
overcorrected freedom approach, 74
overcorrected structure approach, 74
ownership, 23, 94, 141, 154, 190, 192, 199
  of behaviour, 187
  trust and, 189

P

paradigms
  Montessori Paradigm, 17–18
  outdated paradigms, unlearning, 14
  role in education, 14, 16–17
  traditional paradigm, 17
parallel work, 148
parent, 16, 71, 165
  role in Montessori
     homeschooling, 142–143
parent–child connection, 9
parenting, 5, 72, 88, 178
partner involvement in homeschooling,
     40, 41
passive recipients of knowledge,
     children as, 16–17
patience, 19, 61, 153, 207
pedagogy, Montessori as, 178
  individualized vs. personalized
     learning, 180–181
  what adapting does mean, 179–180
  what adapting doesn't mean, 178–179

perfection, xiv, 63, 67, 73, 92, 96, 181–182
  letting go of, 189–190
perfectionism, 14, 30, 134
performance-based thinking, 155, 158
permissive adults, 197
personal responsibility, 18, 102
philosophy. See Montessori philosophy
physical independence, 187
physical science and chemistry, 102
pillars of Montessori, 59
  child, 60
  environment, 61
  guide, 60–61
  importance of, 62
Pink Tower, 100, 121
Pinterest, 55, 86, 96, 108, 123, 142, 212
planes of development, 26, 50, 83, 212
  first plane of development, 3, 26, 78,
     81, 101, 194
  fourth plane of development, 79
  multiple, 94
  second plane of development,
     79, 102
  third plane of development, 79
plug-and-play curriculum, xiv, 31, 111
plug-and-play resources, 108, 142
practical life, 35, 100, 107, 147
  in daily rhythm, 188–189
  integration, 36
  starting with, 92
  trays, 117
Practical Life album, 112
practical life lessons, 147
prepared adult, 9, 20, 50, 66, 130, 176, 179,
     182, 186, 202, 212. See also adult
prepared environment, 5, 6, 36, 73, 80,
     87, 157, 180, 187, 194. See also
     environment
  adult as creator of, 67–68
  creating, 19
preparedness, 181–182
  accessibility versus, 91
presence, 10, 44, 130–131
presentation, 106–107, 135, 138, 143,
     168, 183, 194
preventative discipline, grace and
     courtesy as, 198

primary years, Montessori subjects in, 100
   culture, 101
   language, 100–101
   mathematics, 101
   practical life, 100
   sensorial, 100
principles of Montessori, 179
process over product, importance of, 147–148
productive struggle, 59
progress in Montessori, measuring, 142
purposeful activity, 96, 131, 193

Q

qualification, 24

R

real-life integration, 9
real Montessori environment, xvi, 92–93
real Montessori families, 6
real Montessori homeschooling, xvi
real-world application, 82, 103
reasoning mind, 79
refinement, 149–150
relationships, 27, 42, 102, 162
repetition, 100, 157, 198
   child's path to mastery, 168–169
   observation and, 169–170, 172
resistance, 156–157
respect for the child, 5, 6, 24
respect in Montessori, 44
responsibility, xviii, 55, 73, 75, 142, 154, 155, 157, 186, 189, 191, 199
   flexibility and, 178
   personal, 18, 102
restlessness, 27, 206
rhythm, 27, 83, 86, 125, 149, 176. *See also* daily rhythm; intentional social rhythm, building
   consistent rhythms, establishing, 92
   core values, defining, 126–127
   expectations vs. tasks, 128–130
   family rhythm, 179
   leading with presence, not pressure, 130–131
   three-hour work cycle, 127–128
   using anchors to support transitions, 130
role model and mentor, adult as, 68

S

sandpaper letters, 4, 28, 117, 120, 135, 139, 172
schedules, 16, 131
school-at-home, xviii
   Montessori homeschooling vs., 16
scope and sequence in Montessori, 28, 106, 111
secondhand Montessori materials, buying, 121
second plane of development, 79, 102
Séguin, Édouard, 139
self-awareness, xvii, 15, 19, 61, 69
self-care stations in Montessori, 186, 188
self-construction, 8, 32, 60, 137, 176
self-corrective, 116
self-directed learners, xvi, 18, 97, 194–195
self-directed work, 95
self-discipline, 7, 18, 88, 97, 103, 187, 194–195, 199
self-doubt, 7, 14, 23, 29
self-initiated research, 103
self-paced learning, 8, 36
self-reflection, 81
self-regulation, 18, 97, 154, 195, 197
self-reliance, 191, 214
sensitive periods, 4, 78, 80–82, 137, 138, 194, 203
sensorial learning, 99, 100, 120
sequence in Montessori, 111
shelf, role of, 97
   first shelves, setting up, 98–99
   independence, 98
   thematic shelf, 93
   transition shelf, 99
shelf works, 119, 148
short-and long-term intentions, defining, 35–36
short online workshops/conferences:, attending, 118
simplicity, 37, 96, 98, 107
skill
   motor, 66, 169
   observation, 216
   strengthening, 203
smart material choices, making, 116–117
snack time outdoors, 147
social connections, 164
social-emotional growth, 161, 164, 166, 198

socialization in a Montessori
        homeschool, 25, 162
    mixed-age experiences, facilitating, 163
    neighborhood outreach, 163
    nervous system, 164
    organic play opportunities,
        creating, 163–164
    social connections, 164
    weekly social rhythm, designing, 163
    whole child perspective, 165
social justice, 82
social rhythm, 163
social self, 79
soft skills, 147
sorting activities, 117
sound games, 4
Stamp Game, 120, 146, 148
standardized curriculum, 52, 109, 111
structure and flexibility, balance
        between
    creating a daily rhythm, 125–131
    freedom within limits, 71–75
substitutes, 122
success, 17, 52
supplements, 113, 122
support, 43
supportive community, joining, 118

T
tasks
    cosmic task, 88
    expectations vs., 128–130
    support and, 43
teacher, 52, 53, 54, 96, 136, 150
teacher-created albums, 109–110, 118
teacher training, 119
teaching, 16, 66, 97, 173, 178
    facilitating vs., 19
thematic shelf, 99
thinking
    abstract, 81, 101, 102
    critical, 18, 57, 81
    performance-based, 155, 158
third plane of development, 79
three-hour work cycle, 27, 127–128, 203

Three-part cards, 116
three-period lesson, 92, 139–140
Timeline of Life, 121
timelines, 102
    additional, 121
    external, 26
    internalized, 26
toddlerhood, 154
traditional education, 52
traditional education and Montessori,
        comparison of, 52–53
    adult, role of, 53
    curriculum and pace, 54
    environment, 54–55
    learning process, 53–54
    motivation and assessment, 55
traditional paradigm, 17
traditional schooling, 17, 18, 19, 21, 57
    limitations of, 16
    paradigm, 14
traditional teaching, 16
training center albums, 110
transitions, 130, 158, 204
transition shelf, 98, 99, 147
trust, 19, 149
    as the foundation of independence, 191
    and ownership, 189
trust-building language, 189

U
unconscious absorption, 3
understanding, 92
uninterrupted work cycle, 203–204
unity, creating an environment of,
        44–45
"unsocialized homeschooler," myth of, 162
unstructured play, 163
upper elementary
    adaptation tip, 150–151
    Montessori tips for beginners, 141–142

V
values of Montessori homeschooling,
        6, 34, 40–41
video demonstrations, watching, 118

W

Week 1 of Montessori homeschooling
 consistency and focus, prioritizing, 148–149
 cycle of work, introducing, 148
 observing without intervening, 148
weekly social rhythm, designing, 163
whole child perspective, 165
wholeness, 165
"why" statement, 31, 36–37
 clarity, 31–32
 core values for homeschool, 34
 homeschool mission statement, creating, 34
 ideal day, visualizing, 35
 Montessori aligning with, 36
 practical exercises for defining, 34–36
 reflective prompts to clarify, 33

short-and long-term intentions,
 defining, 35–36
in what's best for the child, 32–33
wonder, 27, 29
Words/Grammar Boxes, function of, 120
workbooks, 8, 16, 165
work cycle in Montessori, 55, 148,
 149, 190–191
 homeschool work cycle, 190–191
 three-hour work cycle, 27, 127–128, 203
 uninterrupted work cycle, 203–204
work in progress, adult as, 69
workspace, dedicated, 97

Z

zoology and botany, 102